The True You
Tools to Excavate, Explore, and Evolve

Jennifer M. Blair

iUniverse, Inc.
Bloomington

The True You
Tools to Excavate, Explore, and Evolve

iUniverse books may be ordered through booksellers or by contacting:

iUniverse
1663 Liberty Drive
Bloomington, IN 47403
www.iuniverse.com
1-800-Authors (1-800-288-4677)

ISBN: 978-1-4620-6260-7 (sc)
ISBN: 978-1-4620-6262-1 (hc)
ISBN: 978-1-4620-6261-4 (e)

Library of Congress Control Number: 2011919355

Printed in the United States of America

iUniverse rev. date: 12/20/2011

"Jennifer Blair is lively, sensitive and insightful. She asks the right questions and provides suggestions that are consistently thoughtful, helpful and reflective of the best in contemporary life coaching. She is an effective model for wit, style and resiliency, and her book, **The True You***, is a compilation of her best work."*

Anita P. Barbee, MSSW, Ph.D. Professor and
Distinguished University Scholar
Kent School of Social Work University of Louisville

"I met Jennifer through an amazing woman I was trying to hire that really impressed me. I wanted to know how she 'was who she was' and learned her best friend was a Life Coach named Jennifer Blair. I absolutely had to have Jennifer's contact information, and since that time in 2004, I've been coaching with Jennifer ever since—it's been life changing!

Jennifer is a truly gifted and incredible person, who will stop at nothing to lovingly help people uncover their true selves, their talents and their greatness. She has supported me in rediscovering my Divine authentic power, helped raise my consciousness in a non-judgmental and loving way with clarity, intention, and the gift of digging beneath my words, asking questions that help me to uncover my inner truths. I now live with inner power, passion, speaking my truth and walk the path with beauty. It has been a gift to my soul to reconnect with my sacred and honor it. I use my values that Jennifer helped me to unearth for every major decision in my life, and as a reminder of who 'I' am. Since I began coaching with Jennifer, I know anything is possible with her guidance and support. Jennifer just 'gets it'."

Susan Swek, Group Chief Designer—Color + Material Design, Ford
Motor Company

"I started my entrepreneurial journey with the launch of Underwired Magazine in September 2006. For anyone who has traded in a steady paycheck in order to take a leap of faith, you know the terrain can be rocky. Couple this with the fact that I chose an industry where 80 percent of new publications fail in the first year, and sleepless nights were plentiful. I soon found myself stuck in the mindset of, 'Why did I think I could do this?'

A colleague who had worked with Jennifer suggested I give coaching a try. My response was a polite, 'no thanks'—my idea of coaching conjured up visions of someone shouting into a microphone in front of a room full of paid attendees, with everyone getting a pitch to buy land in Florida at the end of the evening. I would not have celebrated my fourth year as publisher of Underwired Magazine, a career for which I am wickedly passionate, had I not worked with Jennifer. Life coaching provided the clarity, confidence and grounding that I needed in order to be successful in moving my company forward. Jennifer helped take what was in my head (and heart)... All the big picture ideas I had for Underwired and helped me push through the work necessary to make those dreams a reality. I wasn't scared of the hard work, but rather doubted my ability to make those big ideas happen.

With Jennifer's guidance, I tackled the challenges that come with building a business and learned how to grow from what is presented to me, often having turned adversity into advantage. Conversations were comfortable, confidential and eye-opening. Jennifer was able to guide me to my own answers within, but sometimes it is not enough to know the answer or the way to proceed. You still have to take action around it in order for things to change and with Jennifer; I knew I had someone to hold me accountable and to push me forward.

The entrepreneurial road is still full of ups and downs, but after working with Jennifer, I no longer approach it from the mindset that I can't do it. The magazine is thriving, and I now operate under the mindset that I can achieve anything, fully believing that the possibilities are limitless.

Jennifer has been instrumental in the success of this publication as my Life Coach, a contributing writer, inspirational speaker for our 'Wired and Inspired' events and model for how she lives her own life. I know that you will feel inspired while reading this book."

Laura Grinstead, Publisher, *Underwired* Magazine

To my incredible children with much love, Taylor and Tess. You amazingly remain true to yourselves… I am often in awe.

Contents

The following chapters are a compilation of "Evolve" columns published in Underwired Magazine in Louisville, Kentucky, from May 2007 through September 2011. A cross reference of life themes by chapter is located in the back of the book.

Acknowledgments

There are many people who have supported me in writing this book over the past several years. Some are still in my life, others have moved on… but to every one, I am eternally blessed by having experienced your inspiring goodness. With deep gratitude and appreciation, I want to directly thank the following for their encouragement, love and support:

The writing opportunity: Much gratitude to *Underwired* Magazine editor and publisher, Laura Grinstead, who gave me the platform in 2007 to create and write a monthly Life Coaching column called "Evolve." I am appreciative of your vision in creating such a beautiful magazine that encourages women to pursue their meaningful work and other passionate endeavors. Thank you for having faith in not only my writing and coaching skills, but also my ability to inspire fans with my written and spoken words. I now love writing under deadlines and am grateful to you for the chance to continually raise the bar on my creativity. To Danielle Hammond, our design director, who made all those words fit on the page and still look gorgeous, especially when I insisted that nothing could be cut: thank you. And to the readers of the "Evolve" column, I appreciate your generous feedback, kind words and the brave, empowered lives you are creating.

My coaching world: Thank you to the many leaders I have experienced through the Coaches Training Institute (CTI), especially Jeff Jacobson, Rick Tamlyn and Myrna Jones. To my other earlier CTI colleagues, Robin Jones, Vicki Harley and the late Cheryl Glassner, I have gratitude for your guidance, especially in the earlier years of building my business. And to my 2006-2007 CTI Moose classmates for your unique leadership qualities and generous feedback that allowed me to expand and grow during our program together… I learned so much from each of you and was forever positively changed. A special note of gratitude for James Melcher, who has become one of my dearest friends and supporters, what a gift to have such a heartfelt connection and lifelong friendship.

My amazing support team: To my dazzling coach and CTI leader, Lauren Powers, who makes me laugh, reminds of my bigness, keeps it real and pushes me to remember to believe in myself when doubt sets in…. I am forever grateful. My assistant Meredith Williams keeps me personally and professionally organized-much love to you. I thank my copy editor, Tracy Harris, for the detailed and timely feedback on this manuscript. Thanks to my photographer Lana Rayhill for making me look beautiful to the world, as well as my graphic designer, Natalie Biesel, who translates my ideas into useful, visually classy coaching exercises and materials.

My soulful supporters: To my sister, Michelle Blair Coslik, who is always here for me, loving me through every challenge, big and small, as well as each celebratory success, I am forever grateful for your brilliant insights, off-the-chart creativity, spiritually-grounded perspectives and our "soul sister chats." To my best friend Valerie Jacobs—without her "rock star" smarts, creative collaboration, unending column ideas and loving feedback, I could not imagine this book existing. To Anita Barbee for your wisdom, inspiration, and "hand-holding," I thank you for staying with me on my journey for so long— I am grateful. And, to Maggie Cassaro whose unending support of my purpose and mission, as well as your personal reminders that "I am okay for today," I am grateful you keep me moving forward.

To my husband Frank Shiels who joined me more recently on this journey, I am grateful for your keen interest, creative solutions, fresh perspectives, but mostly your quiet whispers of love and encouragement to "get it done." I love you.

To my family, with immense honor and gratitude to: my brother-in-law, Stephen, who helped me start my own journey to transformation and continues to inspire me. To Avery and Isabella, who aren't quite sure what it is that do, but think I am the coolest Aunt anyway, I love your unconditional support. To my creatively-talented children, Taylor and Tess, who have brainstormed ideas over meals, edited my columns, patiently waited for their needs to be met while I was coaching and writing, I thank you for your patience, love, support and the warm chocolate chip cookies. To my ex-husband, Todd, thank you for supporting my adventure with sound advice and extra support for our children. And to my step-dad, John, I am thankful for your faith and love.

And finally to my mom, Shirley—I am awed by your own strength and perseverance and thank you for modeling how to be a successful entrepreneur, for believing in the importance of my work, for encouraging my creativity (especially telling me how wonderful all of my columns were, even when they weren't) and for your continual, loving support.

And most of all, to my amazing clients for sharing your hopes, dreams, wishes, fears, deepest desires and truest version of yourself with me. I am forever impacted by your bold bravery and passionate pursuit of your fabulous lives. Thank you for including me on your journey and allowing me to compassionately learn from each of you.

Introduction

I admit it… I suffer through writing. Yes, sometimes it is hard for me to sit down and put the words on paper to explain a particular point or convey the exact thoughts regarding a specific life lesson that I am inspired to share. Maybe it's my perfectionist tendencies, my fear no one will benefit from what I have to share—or because it's just downright vulnerable and scary. Other times, I just don't feel like sitting at a computer, cranking out another column or chapter because I would rather spend time connecting to the people I love or experiencing all that life has to offer outside of my home.

Yet, I can't NOT do it. I find writing and the resulting impact of the permanence of words to be exhilaratingly inspiring, personally challenging and powerfully creative. Writing allows me to dance with life and to commit to claiming what I believe. It keeps me moving toward deeper learning and synthesizing from the experiences I encounter so I can continue to grow myself, my clients and my audiences into their personal best.

The True You: Tools to Excavate, Explore & Evolve is a compilation of my life coaching columns that were published for four and a half years in *Underwired* Magazine, a local publication in Louisville, Kentucky. Launched in September 2006, *Underwired* Magazine was designed to support women in their pursuit of meaningful work, creative passion and other spirited adventures. Therefore, when editor and publisher Laura Grinstead approached me in creating a column that supports the magazine's purpose and vision, it made sense.

Created to inspire and motivate people to be the best versions of themselves, the premise for the "Evolve" column was to take my life coaching experiences coupled with insightful life lessons and then write a thought-provoking and action-inspired message based on the magazine's monthly theme. Nine months after the magazine's first issue, the "Evolve" column debuted in April 2007, thereby starting my writing career as a published columnist and now author.

The book you are about to read includes 53 consecutively published columns, as well as additional life coaching exercises and guidelines. These essays and exercises will help you journey into your self, uncover your authenticity and use that wisdom to create a fantastic life. *The True You* represents and reflects what I have learned from my life coaching work with hundreds of clients who have been willing to include me on their path of discovery, as well as the accumulation of my personal life lessons.

I began this part of my journey over ten years ago when I decided to make a major life change. I had been a stay-at-home mom, wife and community volunteer for many years when my marriage fell apart. I decided to embrace the lessons at hand and find a new life direction and purpose. This journey led me to rediscover the part of myself I had lost, the real me that had been covered up for many years.

I spent the next several years retooling, recalibrating, rebalancing and relearning how to make the best choices for myself that led me to not only heal myself, but also to create a new career assisting others to do the same. Over time I came to believe I had a powerful message to share with others. In 2003, I discovered life coaching and I completely resonated with the forward-moving, self-empowering and passion-pursuing modality that could assist others in discovering their own greatness and make BIG life changes. After completing the accredited course work within a few months, I created my company, Excavive™ Life Coaching, as a way to empower people, especially women, to pursue their passions, increase their self-confidence, and build the kind of lives they truly want to live. "Excavive" means to excavate your life, and that is exactly what I do with others through my life coaching, inspirational speaking and writing.

The True You is a book that offers you an opportunity to excavate, explore and evolve into new possibilities and a more fulfilling life. Common themes that appear throughout the book are: authenticity, creativity, beauty, effective communications, emotional clarity, breaking down barriers, empowerment, extreme self-care, fun and play, gratitude, healthy relationships, life balance, abundance, inspired action, overcoming fear, passion, setting goals and spirituality. Through understanding ourselves and how we feel about and behave relative to these ideas, we can excavate, explore and evolve.

While reading this book, you might find it helpful to think about the following terms from the Excavive perspective: "Excavating" means digging into your truths, defining who you are, naming your values and claiming your life purpose. "Exploring" can be defined as giving yourself permission to experiment with new perspectives, going outside the box and taking action for the sake of learning what works and what doesn't for you. And finally, "Evolve" means confidently claiming who you have become and then sustaining those authentic changes.

It is my belief that if you uncover your essence, the deeper part of who you really are, define what is important to you and courageously take inspired action towards your dreams and desires, then you will evolve into the best version of you. You will be free to boldly explore all that life has to offer, breaking down any barriers along the way, and then live life with meaning, passion and purpose.

As I said earlier, my life (and life experiences) evolved into my life's work. Just as the magazine's themes were unveiled each month, I was amazed at how life moved along in a parallel fashion. It seemed as if whatever topic was at hand, there were issues going on in my life or my client's lives that allowed me to write from the context of life's immediate experiences. Through this process of writing and coaching, I quickly learned, life isn't about making huge changes all at once, but rather a variety of changes, big and small, that add up to a transformation. These columns focus on life's everyday challenges and then everyday changes you can make to move your life forward.

It is my hope that you will consider my experiences; incorporate the lists where helpful and engage in the inquiring coaching questions and exercises. As a provocateur for change, it is my job is to help others discover what's right for them by assisting them in excavating their authenticity, seeing their beauty from within and creating their definition of success. I challenge you to form YOUR opinions and take bold action to create congruency in who you are and how you portray that in the world.

Feel free to approach *The True You* moving from beginning to end, or simply pick out the chapter that is most needed in your life right now based on the theme in the Contents section. I have also created a cross reference of themes and chapters which is located in the back. There is no right or wrong way to best utilize this book— it is simply a tool for inspiration, transition and transformation. French novelist Anatole France said, "If the path be beautiful, let us not ask where it leads." Enjoy the journey, open your heart and soul and allow your world to expand.

The *Authentic* Wonder Woman

May 2007

In thinking about women of today, I am amazed at how incredible women are. Women have businesses or careers, manage households, raise children, connect with romantic partners, work out and take care of themselves, spend time with friends, volunteer to worthwhile projects and organizations, indulge in hobbies, participate in book and supper clubs, save the world, attend church and Bible Studies, create art and music, go to social functions… all while trying to achieve balance, poise and grace. It is amazing they can play so many different roles and still have time to accomplish so much. Yet, I wonder, are they happy? Can they really do it all and maintain a life of balance and pleasure? And, are they being the truest version of their authentic selves?

On the outside looking in, most women look and act like they have it all together, and many do. Yet, they often believe that something is often missing… more fun, more passion, more authenticity, more meaning, more love, more joy, full-out permission to be genuine. They are powerful and can be ambitious, yet real women rarely work on acquiring more things, making more money or obtaining more power for the sake of their egos and self-worth. They want their insides to match their outsides and to be fully transparent. The women of today long to maintain their personal power, use it for good in the world and at the same time be completely fulfilled and happy. They are the Authentic Wonder Women (AWW) of modern times.

In my Life Coaching business, I am hired by mostly women to help them rebalance and re-prioritize their lives; re-discover who they are; and reclaim their own inner beauty, passion and self-worth. We create a partnership for re-learning of the self, and we engage in a very powerful process that is energizing, inspiring, accountable and forward moving.

To assist people in finding their true selves, we start by defining a person's values, or the qualities that are most important to them. We excavate their inner depths, and then look at how well they are living their values in each of the basic areas of their lives. It is an opportunity to explore not only what is missing, but also see what's working. Some of the more common values we unearth are around adventure, freedom, beauty, belonging, creativity, helping or impacting others, connection, integrity, trust, fun, learning, love, passion, peace and harmony, and responsibility. The values are the "checklist" for the AWW, and underlie everything we do. I always suggest laying a good foundation for your home before picking out wallpaper… this is what knowing your values does for you.

Once a woman knows what is valuable to her, she can begin to make choices about what she does and how she does it, based on her own guiding principles. That is when the change begins to take place and we start to accomplish what has previously been thought of as impossible. The AWW starts to feel more confident and more beautiful, and acts accordingly. She feels more love for herself and others, and it shows.

The AWW of today is the woman who is real in all of her many roles, and makes the most of her life. She can balance the daily life demands while finding pleasure in all she is doing. It is a choice, and she understands that. Ultimately, every AWW develops common traits, as I have observed below.

The *Authentic* Wonder Woman of today:

Knows her Passion and Purpose The AWW knows what is essential and why she is doing something, and she pursues it with passion. She cultivates creativity, infuses life with fun, and takes inspired action every day.

Connects to Others The AWW is all about tending to her important relationships. A quick phone call, a hug and kiss, making a date to spend time together, a simple "how are you?" She connects and loves.

Asks for What She Wants The AWW understands she is responsible for getting what she needs, being courageous and bold in asking for it and using her voice. She also knows when not to ask, as sometimes there is power in what she does not say!

Practices Gratitude The AWW is thankful for all she has and does. She honors her beliefs and those of others, and constantly recognizes how blessed her life is, even when there are bumps in the road.

Makes Mistakes The AWW recognizes the growth and learning opportunity in every misstep. She doesn't take herself too seriously and laughs A LOT.

Empowers and Helps Others The AWW inspires others by being who she really is. She reaches out to others and wants more for them than for herself.

Rejuvenates Herself The AWW feeds her soul. She prioritizes her time and gets grounded every day. She knows the importance of exercising, nourishing, sleeping, playing, meditating, praying, journaling, beautifying, spending time in nature, creating, reading, and stopping...whatever nurtures her body, mind and spirit.

The Authentic Wonder Woman of our time is powerful beyond belief. When all women start to recognize their own magnificence, they will transform others as well. AWW can play many roles or choose various positions when desired. It only matters that they are being true to themselves and those around them while in those different roles. Females become a true Wonder Woman of today when they have mastered their own authenticity.

Coaching Questions to Discover the *Authentic* Wonder Woman Inside of You:

The following questions below are to get you thinking about how you can tap into your Wonder Woman within. Start a journal or write these answers in a special book that inspires you.

1. When was the last time you experienced true wonder? Describe the peak experiences that have made you the happiest, and look for any common themes.

2. What **unique** values, strengths or skills do you have that directly support your authenticity? Name at least three.

3. What distractions exist in your life that keeps you from being your authentic self? List the things you do instead of being fabulous. (Yes, laundry can be included!)

4. What rituals do you engage in, or desire to create, that would give you permission to fully take care of yourself?

5. When do you hold yourself as powerful, whole and big in the world?

(See "Excavating Your Thoughts: Journaling to Your Authentic Self" in the Appendix.)

Frolic, Fun & Play... Every Day

June 2007

"The world is your playground. Why aren't you playing?"
Ellie Katz

Summer is here! A time that is relaxed, carefree, lazy and unstructured. It is the perfect time to frolic and play and have fun every single day. Frolic is defined as playful behavior or action, merriment, gaiety, fun... so how much fun are you really having? Are you taking time to build play into your life, every day, all year?

People often wait until the weekend or a vacation but you can start now, especially since summertime gives us a jump-start. School is out. The pool is open. Trips are taken. Movies are watched. Books are read. Lemonade stands pop up. Gardens are tended. Parks are filled with people playing sports, taking walks, riding bikes or listening to concerts. Families reunite. It is a time for celebrating, being in the moment and taking breaks from the routine of our lives.

People from across the nation come to me for various reasons in my Life Coaching practice. Some are seeking answers regarding their careers, making more money, setting new goals, or finding the right person. And even though these desired changes are important, I often learn that the key missing element in their lives is not having enough frolic, fun and play... not the better job or different relationship.

The truth is when you focus on play and enjoyment you can create more overall happiness in your life. My clients tell me their reasons for not delving into their true passions are because: "I don't have enough time;" "I don't have enough money;" "I don't have anyone to do that with;" or "I will do that *someday*." I believe these are just excuses and stories. So I say to them, "If not this, what?" and "If not now, when?" It's time you have more of what you want by creating more playful opportunities each and every day.

Here are some ideas for infusing more fun in your life:

Love Being Alive Savor your everyday experiences… I wake up every morning and start the day off by saying "I am so happy and grateful that…" Fill in your own blanks.

Know Your Passions I love Salsa Dancing (at least one to two times weekly!), Rollerblading, walking in the park, snow skiing, dinner and drinks with friends, and chocolate chip cookie dough. Create your own list, and include something new and exciting.

Laugh or Smile 25 times per day It can be infectious to others!

Choose your Playmates Who can I get to play with me today? Maybe it is someone old, new or just you!

Have "Fun Money" Hide money in your wallet. My mother used to give me a $100 bill for my birthday on occasion and say, "Keep this with you in your billfold for something special and spontaneous."

Schedule a "Pajama Day" Take a day off, for real! Stay home in your PJs for 24 hours! You deserve a break from being "on-the-go." I do this at least once a month, and my children love it!

Be Spontaneous and Open to new People, Places and Things Try a new restaurant. Take a class, just for fun. Make a new friend. Travel somewhere new every year. My best friend enjoys playing bocce ball and singing karaoke.

Engage in Nurturing Activities What feeds your body and soul? Spend time in nature, alone and with those you love. Personally, I enjoy massages!

There is no time to waste and YOU are in charge of creating your own playtime. Fun is a conscious choice. It is about giving yourself permission with both your thoughts and your actions to be happy and to enjoy life in the process of it unfolding. Frolicking and fun are different for everyone, so determine what you want. Decide to be happy every day, and then do the juicy, simple or perhaps bold things that will bring you exuberance, passion and pleasure.

Coaching Questions to Inspire More Frolic, Fun & Play:

1. What activities have heart and soul meaning for you?

2. What excuses do you use, or stories you create, that keep you from doing the things you really want to do?

3. What areas of your life need more succulence and joy? Consider your friendships, love life, children, nature, adventure life, your body, family and spirituality.

4. How can you pamper yourself today?

Be Tempted and Do Something About It

July 2007

> "Unfulfilled desires are dangerous forces."
> Sarah Tarleton Colvin

What tempts you? Maybe it is the latest get-rich-quick scheme you read about on-line. Maybe it's sex, power or prestige. Or possibly it's money, possessions or a favorite dessert. When most people hear the word "temptation," it stirs up thoughts of a wild torrid affair, a piece of chocolate, playing hooky, or taking a spontaneous trip where you leave it all behind.

In our Judeo-Christian culture we often hear the Bible verse, "Lead us not into temptation, but deliver us from evil." So, I ask, does temptation always lead us to evil and are the things you want bad? Temptation has a bad reputation, and maybe for good reason, as sometimes there can be devastating consequences to the choices and actions made. But I believe the things people want are not bad, it's the context or circumstances in which they want them. And it can inform them about a deeper holistic desire.

So, what do you want? What if you could be curious about the desire that has ignited within you? What if you could embrace the yearning long enough to see if the current opportunities can lead you into new growth? Maybe longing for passion is pointing you toward more intimacy with your partner. Wanting a new job could be about the desire for more freedom and autonomy. Perhaps your temptation is simply about the need to connect to yourself.

Part of my coaching technique allows me to help my clients examine their beliefs so they can make decisions about what to do with the things they crave most. Beliefs are created based on experiences and relationships, as well as how people are shaped by family, teachers, religious or spiritual leaders, media and books. There are "rules" to play by, but sometimes even those need to be examined so that you can mature and discover your true authenticity. Beliefs are not good or bad; they either limit you and hold you back or empower you and move you forward. Here are my thoughts around being tempted and doing something about it to move forward.

Guidelines on Following Your Desires:

Wake Up to what is being awakened within… What passions need to be expressed? What or who is stirring your soul so much so that you feel like you are doing exactly what you are supposed to be doing?

Follow Your Urges Take chances, activate courage and try something new just for the sake of it. Say "yes" as often as possible.

Be Conscious about your decisions. You are always in choice, even if it is simply in your attitude and thinking. And, don't let FEAR be in charge.

Know Your Line Be fierce for you and what you stand for. Stay true to yourself, and don't compromise. Say yes when you mean yes and no when you mean no. Also, know that you can move your line… just know how far and why you are moving it.

Follow Your Intuition Get quiet and let your body inform you. When we experience a sense of peace and comfort in our bodies, we are in alignment with our thoughts, feelings and decisions.

Cause No Harm to yourself, others or your surroundings. There is no room for living a life of guilt or creating future amends for yourself.

Savor Your Current Life Find joy and appreciate all that you have and do. Feel the textures and see the palette of colors before you. You might discover something new that already exists.

My clients tell me about their temptations and are often looking for someone to give them permission to follow their passions and dreams, to do something different. I give 100 percent full permission after making sure they are truly honoring themselves. I say go for it AND take 100 percent responsibility for your choices and actions. I am not here to judge. I leave that up to my client and their conscience, sacred contracts, and commitments made with self, God and others. I am simply a catalyst for awareness and authentic action.

Coaching Questions to Tempt Authenticity:

1. What is enticing and tantalizing enough to take big risks for your own happiness?

2. What is the distinction between feeling good and being fulfilled?

3. What are the "beliefs" or "rules" you have that are no longer serving you?

4. List five things you truly desire, and give in to your temptations.

(See the "Excavive™ Permission Slip" in the Appendix.)

Take a Chance on YOU

August 2007

> *"If you risk nothing, then you risk everything."*
> Geena Davis

Taking chances in life is often equated with taking risks, being reckless, or rolling the dice, like it is a game to be played. Being successful by taking a chance is often considered a 50/50 probability of something working out the right way, based on the favor or dependency of others, being in the "right" circumstances, having good luck, fate, or the generosity of the "Universe" or God, along with a good plan and lots of hard work. It takes struggling through, being brave, taking courageous steps and finally taking the leap.

Getting to the point of finally making decisions, much less taking action, can be so hard. Yet, I believe it can be made easier by starting with YOU: what you believe in and determining what the next right thing is for you, and not basing it on the opinions of others. What if taking a chance can be seen as an opportunity for authenticity and full permission to live in complete integrity by being who you are supposed to be and doing what you are meant to do. Ask yourself, "What do I want?"

Taking a chance on yourself based on knowing a clear path to success and embracing expansive opportunities, rather than reckless risks, is about saying yes to you first… opening yourself up to the adventure of your life, thinking bigger, following the openings that are presented. It is acting with clarity, self-confidence, faith and a knowingness of doing the right thing for the right reasons in spite of the fears that inevitably arise. When you take a genuine chance, you can ignite the feeling of freedom within yourself and reveal the opportunity to recreate and claim who you really are. Perhaps the "shortcut" to success is getting out of your own way, giving up the illusion of being in control, giving up what others think about you and letting go of fear as much as possible.

The process of Life Coaching is about moving you forward in any area of your life. From career and relationship changes to simply having more fun and creativity, my job as a Life Coach is to help you determine what you want and then look for what keeps you from actually being able to achieve your dreams. My clients are willing to take chances on themselves only after understanding what is important to them, creating a sense of balance, naming fears and then believing that they deserve to receive all the happiness and blessings in the world. You have to get out of your own way, face your fears and do it anyway. Only then can you take steps to move forward and take a real gamble on believing in yourself. Here are some thoughts on how to get out of your own way and let go.

Take a Chance on Yourself by...

- being real
- deciding what would bring you the most joy
- getting out of the box
- creating a new life to go toward
- expressing your true feelings
- following your heart, not your head
- walking through your fears
- saying what you think and want
- letting go
- asking for help
- breaking a self-imposed rule when it no longer serves you
- acting on full faith
- practicing forgiveness
- experiencing and loving someone who seems unlikely
- releasing the outcomes
- trusting it will work out
- being wildly happy
- giving up the old for the new
- listening to your inner voice
- wanting more for others than for yourself (it comes back to you!)
- failing and starting over, if needed

Take a chance on you, your values, your abilities and not the opinions of others. Search your soul and do what feels right for you... deeply trust that you will not betray yourself if you are in integrity with yourself, others and your faith. And always, always, always… follow your heart.

Coaching Questions to Put You First:

1. Start acting today based on who you want to be tomorrow… how can you be extraordinary now?

2. What is the difference between being selfish and being responsible to yourself?

3. What is creating your reality today…reflecting on your past or looking to your future? How is your fear paralyzing you? List EVERYTHING that scares you and ask yourself if it is really true or not.

4. What are you giving up by not taking inspired action NOW? There is no time to waste.

Make Powerful Choices

September 2007

"The greatest gift you will ever have is your life, and the second greatest gift, which you give yourself, is courage to live it to the fullest. Time goes by quickly, and you cannot take it for granted. Appreciate how far you have come, and give yourself the gift of discovering how far you can yet go."
Dr. Sonya Freidman

What makes you feel good? The fleeting moments, the guilty pleasures, the favorite activities, the silly amusements, the little indulgences? There are many things that you can do to make yourself FEEL better in the moment. Sometimes those things are only temporary or fleeting. But what if those things stop working?

What makes you feel good are your authentic preferences. You must search inside, find your inner truth and make conscious choices. Are you fulfilling your soul's deepest longing and purpose? If your answer is no, why not? Feeling good is a choice AND knowing and believing you have options. You must make decisions based on trusting yourself. Nothing feels better than the freedom to choose what is right for you, to be empowered, to exercise your free will and to let your inner beauty shine through.

People come to me who have become disenchanted by life circumstances or dis-empowered by others based on misunderstandings, lack of communication, financial dependence, seeking approval, trying to keep peace, or not wanting to hurt or disappoint another person. They have become the sum of their life choices, yet they keep making the same mistakes.

I often hear people say, "I don't have a choice." Yet, I believe you do. You get to decide how you show up in the world. Your current circumstances may not allow you to do and get everything you want now, but you can certainly begin to create what is next and make a new plan. In every moment, you are in choice with your thoughts, your feelings, your beliefs, your attitudes and your actions... those are yours and cannot be taken away.

Coaching can help you understand what will ultimately fulfill you, as well as give you the permission, the tools, the communication skills and the freedom to start moving your life forward. The process allows you to create powerful choices and actions based on who and what you want to be, how you want to do something, who you want to do it with and when you want to get started. Choosing an old pattern or behavior can make you feel bad and it denies you the opportunity for transformation and growth. Unless you start exercising your freedom of choice and basking in the beauty that awaits you, you will remain imprisoned, believing you have little control over your destiny or dreams.

<u>The Choice is Yours to...</u>

<u>Be Honest with Yourself</u> Are you feeling good about where you are in your life and who you have evolved into? Are you living the life you truly want to experience?

<u>Keep Your Integrity</u> Don't let someone else's attitudes become yours if they do not ring true for you. What do YOU think? Make your actions and words meet.

<u>Let It Be</u> Don't control, fix or try to change others. Keep the focus on you.

<u>Set Boundaries and Learn to say NO!</u> What others think of you is not your concern.

<u>Change your Mind</u> You have the right to make a different choice based on new information and situations.

<u>Use Your Voice</u> Speak up and ask for what you want. Don't be a doormat or let anyone run over you.

<u>Embrace Self-Care</u> Get your needs met and connect to those you love. Stay grounded.

<u>Be Grateful for What You Have in Every Moment</u> Create a list of everything for which you are thankful.

Choose happiness and joy, purpose and passion, forgiveness and compassion. Examine the energy and impact of people, places and things that currently exist in your life—the good for you versus the bad for you-and choose the good. Decide to say yes to you and no to the bad behavior of others. Choose to live a life that is fruitful, abundant and completely used up in the end. Commit to living your deepest dreams and desires… moment-by-moment, step-by-step… one choice at a time.

<u>Coaching Questions to Get Empowered Around Your Choices:</u>

1. How are you using your voice to say what you want and how you feel? Count the number of times you speak powerfully each and every day until speaking strongly becomes a habit.

2. Notice every time you use the word "should"… is it truly what you want or a different version of what you think you are supposed to do, say, think or feel?

3. Who are the "energy vampires" in your life, and what are you willing to do to make those relationships different? What are you tolerating?

4. Are you being nice or are you being real? (I know this one… I'm a Southern girl!)

(See "Excavating Your Energy" coaching exercise in the Appendix.)

Tap Into Your Feminine Pink Power

October 2007

> "Trusting our intuition often saves us from disaster."
> Anne Wilson Schaef

I love the color pink, always have. My life began in pink when I was wrapped in a pink blanket almost half a century ago (I still have it). In my childhood, I sold pink lemonade, ate pink cotton candy and played in my pink room. Pink sunsets are still awe-inspiring and remind me of the presence of God and the infinite possibilities in this world. I am happy wearing my soft, pink cashmere sweater as I write this column, and am considering purchasing my new laptop in pink because it made me smile when I saw it at the store.

The color of pink has a long history for many people. More recently, it has come to be associated with breast cancer awareness and the importance of compassion, courage and gratitude for life. But more than that, to me, the color pink represents the depth of the feminine senses and power of intuition.

So, how do you tap into your "pink" softer, feminine side and still remain effective in the "navy blue" masculine world of achieving, doing and accomplishing?

I believe you can connect to your femininity by first honoring your senses on a continual basis. The five senses of seeing, hearing, touching, tasting and smelling will help you to tap into your feelings, your thoughts and your emotions. Delighting in your senses will create the awareness of what is right for you.

When you have a keen perception of your initial five senses, you can then awaken your sixth sense, also known as intuition. This powerful intuition is an inner knowing, a small voice inside that allows you to know the truth before you reveal it to the outside world. It is your gut feeling, a place of peace, a sense of harmony and an all-knowing self-trust. Women are often credited with having better instincts, a very feminine trait. Yet, I think everyone can cultivate it. So, use your intuition… it is the height of your feminine power and wisdom.

<u>Tapping Fully Into Your Feminine Power:</u>

<u>Savor "The Five Senses"</u> Find your passions that ignite and expand what you see, hear, touch, taste, and smell. It will set your moods.

<u>Develop Your "Sixth" Sense, Your Intuition</u> Meditate, journal and get quiet. "Listen" to what is revealed. Only you know what is true and right for you.

<u>Embrace Your Feminine Power</u> Love yourself and celebrate your successes.

<u>Schedule White Spaces on Your Calendar</u> Give yourself time to think, daydream, ponder, read, write… all without speaking or being spoken to. Become conscious and aware.

<u>Design Your Sensual Surroundings</u> Find a place of your own that is just for you, where you feel safe, womanly and exquisite.

<u>Let Nature Be Your Guide</u> Go outside and observe. Breathe and smell the fresh air. Choose the scenic routes.

<u>Live Your Life in Color</u> Use your favorite colors, the ones that truly reflect you and create the impact you want to make.

<u>Wear Divinely Feminine Clothes</u> Embrace any textile that makes you feel good. Wear dresses and skirts. Adorn with jewelry and scarves. Use make-up. AND stop wearing only black!

Let your senses ignite your soul and amplify your overall happiness and pleasure in all of the areas of your life. Begin by putting your heart, mind, body and soul into the small acts of everyday, so they can make up your big ideal life. Engage all the sensations of seeing beauty, tasting sweetness, hearing laughter, touching softness, and smelling aromas. And above all, listen to what is revealed about the poetry of your life through your intuition. It is your true divine power.

Coaching Questions to Embrace Your Feminine Power:

1. Are you living in a way that is deeply satisfying and truly expresses you and your soul? Be sure you are living YOUR life.

2. When you want blissful solitude, what are your uninterrupted escapes that allow you to feel happy and peaceful?

3. What does it feel like to be awed?

4. What would landing more softly in your life look like? In other words, what if your life were easy, light, and playful?

5. How do your physical spaces and environment impact you and how you feel? What colors do you want to see more of? Perhaps, more pink?

Cultivate Your Inner Circle

November 2007

"Wherever we are, it is our friends who make our world."
Henry Drummond

"Each friend represents a world in us, a world possibly not born until they arrive, and it is only by this meeting that a new world is born."
Anais Nin

Have you looked at the company you are keeping lately? Do you like what you see? Are you being honored by the people around you? Are your friendships reciprocal? Is your cup being filled with joy and laughter?

Most people in life want to love and be loved, to see and be seen, to know and be known. Often their "knowingness" comes from a best friend more than with anyone else in their world. Many women long for a place to completely relax into themselves, to take off the masks, and to be accepted for who they really are. They want a place to go, not to be fixed, but simply to feel whole, safe and welcome… a home for their authentic selves.

Best friends help create authentic, deeply connected, intimate relationships. These "soul sisters" provide a playground to experiment with different ways of being, to try out new things, to fully express feelings and emotions, to fail and start over, to speak what is true and real and to cultivate the person they are becoming. Best friend relationships often exhibit the qualities desired for other, sometimes more challenging, relationships with intimate partners, work colleagues or even family members.

Recently, I have listened to many of my coaching clients' frustrations with the quality of their friendships. They have fallen into some bad habits such as not spending time with those important to them; keeping friends who no longer work for them; not setting boundaries; not speaking their truth; or even allowing others decide who their friends are, rather than being proactive by deciding who they want in their inner circles. Many are letting their friendships move to the bottom of the priority list, when it is precisely this camaraderie that makes them feel alive and nourishes them the most.

My suggestion is to choose and cultivate the relationships that enhance your soul for where you are in your life right now. Don't pick your alliances out of circumstances such as work, community service, children's friends, neighbors or even your partner's spouses. Circumstantial friends help to bridge the gap, provide fun and entertainment, and give companionship when others are not available. However, I believe it is best to pick close friends who align with your same values and beliefs. Consciously design a close circle of friends who will support your life and all that you do and dream of doing. Here's how…

Enhance Your Friendships by your Honoring Values:

Listed below are the more prevalent values related to friendships I have unearthed with my coaching clients. I suggest you pick your top ten and rate them in order of importance to you and your needs for your closest friendships. Have your best friends also do this exercise and compare notes! And of course, feel free to add your own qualities, or for an expanded list, see "A Sampling of Values" in the Appendix.

Acceptance
Acknowledgment
Adventure & Exploration
Appreciation
Authenticity
Collaboration
Connectedness
Ease
Encouragement
Flow & Flexibility
Freedom to be self
Fun & Play
Genuine
Happiness
Harmony
Honesty
Humor

Kindness
Kindred spirits
Love
Loyalty
Openness
Peaceful
Reciprocal
Respect
Rewarding
Safety
Spirituality
Stylish
Support
Trust
Understanding

By knowing what is most important to you, you can choose to value yourself and revere those closest to you at the same time. Give yourself the freedom to open your heart with love, and live your own values within a friendship. Look at your life and see who honors you and has stuck by you; reward that person with your full presence. And above all, create the opportunity to grow and expand together through the challenges and joys on the journey of your life by planning the next ten years of your friendship.

Coaching Questions to Consciously Evolve Your Friendships:

1. Who is in your Inner Circle?

2. How do your relationships support your continual evolvement into the best you and who you are becoming?

3. What does it feel like to be truly loved, accepted and encouraged WITHOUT judgment?

4. Who are "they" who hold so much power over you and your life?

5. Who makes you smile and nurtures your soul?

6. If you had a few hours to live, who are the friends you would call? And, why are you waiting?

Let the Power of Listing Serve You... Not Enslave You

December 2007

"Written goals have a way of transforming wishes into wants; can'ts into cans; dreams into plans; and plans into reality. Don't just think it-ink it!"
Dan Zadra

How many lists do you make over and over again? Things to do. Errands to run. Groceries to buy. Work tasks to be completed. Goals to set. Calls to return. School supplies, clothes and gifts to purchase. Home repairs to be scheduled. Vacations to plan…the daily, weekly, monthly and yearly lists can be endless.

I have observed that people's lives are run by their "to do" lists. They make long, detailed lists, often adding an unrealistic number of items to be completed in a short timeframe. I see clients focus on what is not done rather than celebrate what gets completed. When they do finish a job, they are so focused on moving forward to the next item that they give little thought or recognition for a job well done. Their sense of accomplishment, even self worth, is determined by the number items they check off on a regular basis, instead of the quality and balance they are bringing to their overall lives.

Are you being realistic about your lists and the role they play in your life? How many lists do you create, what is on them, and how much time do you allocate? Do you consider if an item really needs to be on the list? Many people sacrifice what is most important to them, such as "me" time to rejuvenate or an occasion to connect with others, simply because they are driven to get one more thing crossed off.

These out-of-control "bad lists" are not good for you, and can create a lot of crazy making. I challenge you to think about how you can be in charge of your lists, your time and your life by simplifying what you do. Let the power of listing serve you, not enslave you.

Three Favorite Listing Habits to Instill:

1. **Brain Dump** Use a blank notepad and write down everything that comes to mind, dump it all. Thoughts, tasks, feelings, goals, dreams, desires. Big or small, anything and everything… this is a mind-clearing. Tuck it away and refer back to it a month later so you can experience the joy of how much you have accomplished without constantly looking at a piece of paper. (See "Brain Dumping" coaching exercise in the Appendix).

2. **"Post-It Note" It** Put each item on a Post-it note, and stick it on the wall. This "displayed thinking" allows you to move items around to group together, to look at what needs to be done next or even see pieces of a bigger picture. It can give you a fresh perspective and help you better organize your thoughts and action items.

3. **Pick Three** Choose only the top three things you want to accomplish each day. It is not necessary to have 25 items on a list, and you can get more done by focusing on what is most important in helping you achieve your goals. Share your "pick three" with your best friend or partner at the end of each day.

Three Lists to Invoke Positivity:

1. **Gratitude List** Write down who and what you are grateful for. Be sure to share it with others. (See "Excavating Your Gratitude" coaching exercise in the Appendix).

2. **Accomplishment List** Make a list of things you have done over the past year so you can see how far you have come. Add to it and embrace your fabulousness. (See "Excavating Your Accomplishments" coaching exercise in the Appendix).

3. **Dream List** Envision your dreams by brainstorming a list, mind-mapping or creating a vision that embraces who you want to be and where you want to go. List your desires through journaling, making vision boards or putting your items in a dream box. Claim what you want.

Transforming your list into something useful and "right-sizing" it relative to the realities of your life will give you a fresh perspective and more success. Follow your rhythm by knowing when you are most productive and align your actions accordingly. Good lists serve as focused reminders, goal setting, next steps and processes, mind de-clutterers, creative outlets or assistance to embracing all that you have and still desire to achieve. Make sure you are in command of your lists and, ultimately, your life.

Coaching Questions to Consider When Creating Lists:

1. How will "this item" move you forward in reaching your goals and connecting you to your bigger life vision?

2. Is there "something" on the list that can be done tomorrow in order to create more space for you today?

3. Where do you need to "out-source" something on your list to be more efficient and effective?

4. Will doing "this task" bring you joy?

Set Your Goals through Soulful Dieting

January 2008

> "When we are motivated by goals that have deep meaning, by dreams that need completion, by pure love that needs expressing, then we truly live life."
> Greg Anderson

The start of a new year is an opportunity to kick off a re-evaluation of life and your current state of affairs- where you have been, where you are now and where you want to go next. This process of setting fresh goals, making new resolutions, reflecting on the previous year's successes and perhaps failures, learning the necessary lessons and setting your sights on what you want to accomplish is often done at the beginning of a new year in the form of grandiose thoughts and big intentions. People embark on grand ideas around the perfect or healthier body, the dream job, a large savings account, a bigger house or the next great adventure: and they invest time, effort and money into pursuing their aspirations.

Setting goals is important in giving meaning and focus to what is next, especially when you are clear about what attaining them will represent for you and others. The problem I have observed in others while setting their new goals often lies not just in being unclear, indecisive or unfocused, but also in not letting go of something else first in order to make room for the new ideas and generate sustainable solutions for what they truly desire. People just start piling on to what they already have, making the lists longer and tasks harder. For example, envision hiking up a mountain with a backpack filled with supplies and collected rocks along the way. Eventually the journey will feel long, hard and exhausting. Instead, they need to stop collecting the rocks (issues or more stuff), clean out what is no longer needed before beginning the journey and then they are able to go the distance with lightness and ease.

In order to make changes in your life, I believe external space needs to be created by letting go of people, places and things that no longer work for you. An inner diet is also needed for the soul to cleanse the emotional baggage and old stories, such as anger, resentment, worries, anxieties, busyness and the "what ifs" that might still be hanging on. It is important to not only tighten up your abs, but also look at your inner emotional landscape to see what needs to be trimmed. By understanding your purpose and being clear about what you will get more of, such as love, joy, passion or security, it will then be easier to move toward soulful achievements. Take a look at your true needs and desires, and then choose "the diet" that will build long-term, healthy lifestyle changes for your body, mind and spirit.

Soulful Life Areas to Get Slim and Trim:

An exercise I use with my Life Coaching clients is a Wheel of Life that examines the level of happiness and satisfaction in eight major life areas. This process provides perspective, balance and focus on where to start trimming the unnecessary "weight" that you might be holding, and start adding in the things you really want. Here are some ideas:

Career & Education Discover what makes you satisfied in your work, set boundaries and make sure the rewards match the job. If not, explore new possibilities.

Money Tighten up wasteful spending habits, unnecessary purchases and re-allocate money for the things you really want to have and experience. Form a healthy relationship with money.

Health & Wellness Trim the internal and external body baggage, change eating habits, give up distractions to rest and relaxation (e-mail, TV or the Blackberry,) increase your physical activities and stop the mental chatter that keeps you stirred up.

Friends & Family Savor your connections by giving as much as you receive. Let the people in your life sustain you and your dreams. And, let go of (or redesign) the friendships that no longer work for you.

Romantic Relationship Melt away old relationships, resentments, patterns and bad habits in order to open your heart to soulful, romantic love. And, if you are single, can you be happy with or without someone in your life?

Personal Growth, Spirituality & Religion Let your faith and beliefs serve you on a daily basis. Give up the ones that hinder you or no longer align with who you have become.

Fun & Play Don't wait for the "somedays." Feed your soul by carving out time to play or learn something new. Choose your playmates and playgrounds.

Physical Spaces What stuff needs to be thrown away, donated or sold in order to open up space for the things you want in your surroundings? If you do not love your physical backdrops, then what changes are you willing to make?

(See the "Wheel of Life" in the Appendix for a visual image of this exercise.)

Soulful Coaching Questions to Excavate Your Sleek Self:

Think about any area of your life that you would like to change. What would you like to accomplish next month? Next year? In five years? Do these goals excite and expand you? Are they soulful intentions? Once you reach your goals, what will they give you? The following questions will assist you in excavating your next best steps to achieving your aspirations.

1. What are the three most soulful goals you desire to accomplish?

2. What are the TOP three things you achieved in _____?

3. Name three things you wanted to accomplish but didn't.

4. If everything is possible, identify <u>ONE</u> thing you'd like to be able to say about your life in one year that you can't say today.

5. What will keep you from reaching your goals? Name "your stoppers."

6. What are you willing to trim from your life in order to have MORE_____ (you fill in the blank... love, passion, time peace, prosperity, etc.)

7. What are three Inspired Actions you can take to get started?

8. What will you do first, and by when?

9. Who will you be accountable to and ask for support?

10. What rewards and splurges will you give yourself not only when you accomplish your goal, but also along the way?

Make-up or Break-up... Either Way, Create a Life to Go Toward

February 2008

> "Each relationship you have with another person reflects the relationship you have with yourself."
> Alice Deville

When is it time to go? When is it best to stay? What drives people to stay in relationships when there is a deep knowing that it does not really work anymore? When are you pleasing others so much that you forget who you are and how to take care of yourself? Without nurturing ourselves and others, eventually, our behaviors and choices can lead to losing people we love and care about very much, whether we are in romantic partnerships, friendships or even professional relationships.

People usually do not break up from a lack of loving each other. Love is not the problem. Break-ups occur for many reasons, some including unmet expectations or needs, poor communication, lack of investment with time or money, extinguished passion, loss of respect, dismissal of each other's dreams, fear of abandonment or loss, the need for control, and even ignorance of how the other person needs to feel loved and cherished.

Beyond these, I believe one of the greatest causes of disconnection is a lack of self-esteem and not recognizing or understanding one's OWN value. People often look to another person to make them feel good about themselves and to get their needs met instead of being in charge of their own self worth. We want others to fill up our tanks instead of getting happy with who we are, what we do and why we are doing it. So, how do you retrieve yourself?

In my Life Coaching practice, I often work with people who are going through or considering life and relational transitions such as divorce or other major break-ups. My clients begin by rediscovering their own significance and then designing a vision of the life they want to lead both personally and professionally. They examine ways in which they can create true intimacy with themselves through self-acceptance, love and reclaiming their own essence. They are then able to connect with others with clarity, empowerment and self-confidence, rather than neediness or lack of self-worth.

In an ideal situation, it is always good when people can work through their differences to become stronger, to create more understanding between each other, and to reunite in the best possible way. Sometimes people work hard work to remain together, yet in the end, one, the other or both people might choose to leave anyway. That is why it is important that no matter whether individuals decide to honor their current commitment; create an exit strategy; or remain open to other possibilities, they need to create a life to go toward.

<u>12 Tips to Transform Yourself and Your Relationships:</u>

1. Say no in order to say yes to YOU.

2. Forgive yourself and others; don't play the "Blame Game."

3. Let go gracefully.

4. Realize today's situation is not tomorrow's reality.

5. Trust your intuition.

6. Create clean closures.

7. Fill your own spiritual void.

8. Launch a new YOU.

9. Date yourself.

10. Learn something new.

11. Pursue your passions.

12. Go where you are celebrated.

In the end, if you break up it can be hard, and yes, very painful. But I do not believe that you have to suffer through it, nor be a martyr to your situation. Saying goodbye to a relationship or situation that no longer works for you is saying yes to you and more possibilities for your own life. A break-up can be an opportunity to grow, learn and transform. When you focus on yourself and truly learn to love who you are, you will become blissfully happy.

Coaching Questions to Retrieve Yourself:

1. Whether you make up or break up, what is your vision for a life you want to go toward?

2. What would your love life look like if you were dating you?

3. What do you want and need in your relationships? Make a list of all of the things you want your partner to do for you, and then ask him or her for what you need or do it for yourself.

Turn Envy Into Action

March 2008

"It seems to me that we can never give up longing and wishing while we are thoroughly alive. There are certain things we feel to be beautiful and good, and we must hunger after them."
George Eliot

Do you spend time thinking about what you don't have and what others do have? Do you imagine "the grass is greener on the other side?" Consider what life might look like if you ended up with another person, could be just like so-and-so, could live somewhere else, or perhaps had more money to live a decadently free life? In other words, do you find that you are at times "green with envy" of other people, places and things?

To some degree, I believe most people want more of something they do not have whether it is materially, relationally, spiritually, financially, emotionally or physically. If not, where would the motivation come from to do better, become better, and accomplish more in order to positively impact ours and the lives of family, friends and communities? Envy can provide the desire to create the best version of self.

Let's look at the people, places and things you might long for...instead of envying other people for who you think they are or the life you see that they lead, why not let the things you are attracted to in another person such as their smile, their kindness or their self-confidence, motivate you to find that within yourself or accept your own uniqueness.

If you crave being in another place, whether it is a trip or a new home, self-check to determine if you are escaping or running away from a situation you do not want to face or you simply long for more beauty. When it comes to the coveting of new possessions, buying something because you think it will bring you more overall acceptance or will help you to fit in is not a good reason for your purchase. But if something you want makes you feel beautiful, confident or happy and you can afford it, then go for it.

Unfortunately, as one of the seven deadly sins, envy does have a bad reputation as it can create resentment and jealousy. Envy is bad when it hurts your self-esteem, causes you to focus on what you lack or it creates any negativity around others' achievements. When it causes you to be a victim and makes you feel inferior, you might be compromising who you are.

Being a martyr to your circumstances is not pretty either, and any of these thoughts could hold you back from creating the life you could have. However, when you learn to recognize the difference between the good and evil of envy, then envy can inspire you into action.

Envy is Good When It…

- Motivates you to learn more about who you really are.
- Crystallizes your own dreams and desires.
- Dismisses mediocrity, inadequacy or fear.
- Teaches you to ask for help from others and to be real, open, honest and vulnerable.
- Offers a new perspective and viewpoint.
- Ignites authentic action.
- Helps you to find mentors and gain knowledge from their successes.
- Builds your confidence by making choices that are true to you.

I believe envy can give you the chance to find out what you truly want. It provides a gauge to see where you rank on your own happiness meter, and it can give you a zeal that creates a drive for enhancement. Envy can cause you to have a conscious life full of choices, and can turn your envy into enthusiastic and rewarding action.

Coaching Steps to Turn Envy into Action:

1. List five things that you truly envy.

2. Using the list above, probe deeper by noticing more specifically what emotions get triggered… are you jealous? Angry? Happy? Sad? Frustrated?

3. Now, what action items are you willing to take to get what you want for yourself that are based on the "right" feelings for you?

4. Ask yourself, will these items create sustainable fulfillment or just happiness in the moment?

5. Now, choose the one that speaks to your heart and soul and do that one first.

Mint Your Abundance:
Cultivate Prosperity

April 2008

> "I gain strength, courage and confidence by every experience in which I must stop and look fear in the face...I say to myself, I've lived through this and can take the next thing that comes along. We must do the things we think we cannot do."
> Eleanor Roosevelt

Abundance can mean different things to different people, and can include both the tangible and intangible areas of life. Concrete achievements like a successful career, a beautiful home, financial accumulation, a great wardrobe and a fit body, as well as the non-physical richness of passion, loving relationships, creative pursuits, a Spiritual connection and serving others are all important. Living abundantly encompasses creating and balancing your definition of wealth relationally, spiritually, mentally, emotionally, physically and financially. The most challenging of these areas for many women is around money and their thoughts about financial success.

All things start with a thought, including your path to prosperity. When I work with my clients, part of the life coaching process includes identifying personal values, beliefs, strengths and talents to create clarity, desire and momentum in achieving goals. It is important to align thoughts about money- what it means to you, how you receive it and what it does for you- in this process. When clients hit a block, it is often in the form of a self-limiting belief or fear that must be turned around in order to keep moving forward. Below are some of the common constraining beliefs around money that I encounter…. and how they can be transformed.

Transforming Scarcity Beliefs into Empowering Action:

"I can't make enough money to support myself doing what I love and am passionate about." If you do what is of service and of value to yourself and others, and you are taking the right actions, the money will show up.

"The Bag Lady Syndrome" Are you living with the daily fear of going broke and ending up living on the streets when TODAY you are okay? Take action as a creative, empowered, and resourceful individual, so that you are in charge of your fate.

"I feel guilty for wanting nice things." If your intent around a purchase is because you love something, it brings you joy and you can afford it, then why not? If it is to impress others or complete a facade, then think again.

"I need to take care of everyone else first, and then I will get to me later." Are you being a victim to your spouse, your children or your friends? If you do not take care of you, then who will? Putting you first by getting pampered, replenished and nourished will enable you to show up fully when you are needed.

"I will do that someday when I have more time and money." What are you waiting for? Life is short and happening now; and you may not get the opportunity, time, money or energy later. Only today is a certainty.

"I can't charge that rate! People cannot afford me and will not hire me." Know your personal value, what you stand for, what the market can bear and who you serve. Put the appropriate value on your products, services, time and talent. Don't expect other people to value you if you do not value yourself.

A Coaching Exercise To Increase Your Abundant Thinking:

Scarcity thinking can be a hindrance and bad habit. When you visualize your success and begin to think abundantly, you can increase your ability to manifest your true aspirations. So, let's practice thinking about possibilities, dreams and desires.

1. If you were to find an extra **$10** today, what would you do with that money? Would you treat yourself to a latte?

2. Now let's multiply that by 10 ... how would you spend **$100**? A special gift or experience for you, your partner or your family?

3. Again, let's 10 times that number to **$1,000**... what would you buy, save or give away?

4. Once more, let's multiply it by 10 and consider what you would do with **$10,000**? A dream vacation, a new career, increased savings, or pay off some debt?

5. Starting with **$100,000**, what's next? Would you pay down your mortgage, put away money for college, retirement, or a business investment?

6. Finally, **$1,000,000** to create your dreams... how would you fully step into living abundantly?

Now, choose your dream and start seeing, feeling, imprinting and believing in your own wealth. When fear, self-doubt or old stories arise, learn to replace the dis-empowerment with new, positive thought patterns and you will begin to appreciate your own greatness. Your soul's desire and true essence will emerge and you will cultivate your own definition of success. Mint your abundance by making it happen, money and all.

Experience Your Full Range of Emotions

May 2008

"Emotion is the chief source of all becoming conscious. There can be no transforming of darkness into light and of apathy into movement without emotion."
Carl Jung

How are you feeling today? Happy? Sad? Glad? Mad? Can you actually name the many swirling feelings that are often going on at the same time? Women are seen as the emotional ones, the backbone of families and organizations. Yet the paradox is that when they fully express those same emotions that make them sensitive, feminine and loving, they are seen as the weaker sex or even incompetent. Women, as well as men, are taught to believe that if they cry then they are not strong, and worse, are seen as feeble, needy, dependent or even fragile. Further, people are often encouraged to suppress their feelings, to toughen up and to ignore their own needs for the sake of appearing stable and consistent. Is that really an authentic way to live?

In my opinion, emotions are not right or wrong; they are simply guides to inform people about what they need to do in order to take care of themselves. When emotions are ignored, it actually causes them to intensify and can create a vicious cycle of unproductive thoughts and unclear actions. Ignoring emotional needs can trigger sadness, anxiety, depression, tiredness, isolation, worthlessness and even physical illness. But by truly experiencing emotions fully and deeply, one can become alive, self-confident, integrated and empowered. Using emotions to be a trusted inner guide will bring happiness, joy and true fulfillment.

A strong, powerful woman can own her emotions, she can name how she is feeling and understands the next best action to take. She is emotionally intelligent and what is often not realized is that she is experiencing many emotions at the same time. Her savvy understanding of this complexity allows her to tease out what is really going on and she knows that by staying with whatever feeling is there, it will pass and she can gain wisdom from that experience.

Encountering a variety of feelings allows her to be more sensitive to others, to speed up and keep moving in the direction that feels good or to slow down and take time off when rest or rejuvenation is needed. Having empathy for others, taking inspired action for needed change, stepping into creative solutions or setting boundaries are all part of an emotionally intelligent way of being with emotions. Having an understanding of a deep complex internal state informs people on how to be happy with whatever is handed to them, then enables them to be proactive to make desirable and necessary changes.

So, are you letting your emotions have a proper place in your life? Are you learning how your emotions impact you, or are you merely suppressing them and keeping your happy face on, even if that is not how you really feel? Become an emotionally smart woman and insist on experiencing a full, rich, expressive life.

Enhance Your Life by Honoring Your Emotions:

Listed below are the more prevalent emotions I have unearthed both personally and professionally. With what emotions are you familiar?

Amazed	*Happy*
Angry	*Hopeful*
Annoyed	*Hopeless*
Anxious	*Hurt*
Ashamed	*Impatient*
Bored	*Inspired*
Cautious	*Irritated*
Concerned	*Jealous*
Confident	*Joyful*
Confused	*Lonely*
Depressed	*Loved*
Disappointed	*Optimistic*

Disgusted	*Overwhelmed*
Ecstatic	*Proud*
Embarrassed	*Relieved*
Enraged	*Sad*
Excited	*Shocked*
Exhausted	*Shy*
Frustrated	*Surprised*
Guilty	*Thankful*

Name, claim and experience as many emotions as possible. Give thought to what learning is available to you and then discover how to be comfortable with whatever arises. Although emotions are fleeting and they do pass, the experience of feeling a wide range of emotions will teach you to be at ease with yourself. The more you allow the feelings to flow through you in the present moment, the more plentiful and more relaxed your life can be.

Coaching Questions to Evoke a Full Range of Emotions:

Using the list of emotions above, answer the following questions. For an expanded list, see "A Sampling of Emotions" in the Appendix.

1. With which emotions are you comfortable?

2. Take a moment to be with any difficult emotions and consider how circumventing them is a way to avoid pain. What are you doing to escape the pain? (Like shopping, eating, relationships, work, exercise)

3. If you are not in charge of your emotions, then who or what is running your life?

4. Which feelings would you engage in if you were living your life powerfully? And, what could you then accomplish?

Create Your Life Adventure: Take a Break

June 2008

"Because of our routines we forget that life is an ongoing adventure."
Maya Angelou

When is the last time you really got away? Where have you been lately that has allowed you to mentally leave your work behind, enjoy time off, relax, create a new memory and really do what you want? As summer begins, there is an opportunity to think about vacations, breaks, pauses, immersions and escaping with children out of school and the hurried-pace of activities slowing down. What purpose do breaks serve and do we really know how to get away?

There is no doubt that taking breaks can nurture the body, mind and soul. Our society supports time off in many different forms such as coffee breaks, weekend getaways, the traditional two to three weeks of vacation time and sabbaticals. People have become especially good at getting out of the daily and weekly grind by engaging in activities that fill up their tanks. Meditating, working out, reading books, being outside, daydreaming, seeing movies, socializing, lunching and dinnering, being alone, creating technology-free zones, planning spa days, taking bubble baths, going on short getaways… these are some of the respites that keep us going.

Yet, I wonder if these smaller activities are enough to truly sustain us? Are we taking the longer breaks that allow us to completely unwind and give us joy, fun, adventure and learning? When it comes to long-term health and happiness, are we balancing the leisure interests, hobbies and grounding tools with the peak experiences and big adventures that produce greater fulfillment?

I am as guilty as everyone else about taking time off. I admit that as a Life Coach, I should know better. I work hard, love what I do and

I am pretty good about maintaining balance, having solitude, engaging spontaneity and vacationing with family and friends. But what I recently realized is when I made a commitment to grow my business, I would go though the motions of time off but not truly take a break from my work.

I became addicted to my "crack berry" and was constantly connected to my efforts. I would think about creative ideas or new coaching exercises and hardly stop to be truly present while on my vacations. When I finally stopped for a ski holiday last year, I set aside everything Excavive™ and was able to fully enjoy my trip by skiing, nurturing my relationships, reading a historical fiction book, drinking wine by the fire and resting. When I returned, I re-prioritized my work/life balance and was able to gain the personal and professional growth I had been seeking. Now, I am planning my next big escape, and I invite you to think about your getaways as well.

With the Busyness of Life, Why Stop and Take a Bigger Time Out?

- to get away from the mundane and routine
- to create self awareness by noticing who you have become
- to find new inspiration and creativity
- to see beauty in your surroundings and situation
- to remember why you made the choices you did
- to avoid burnout
- to check in and see if yesterday's goals still fit tomorrow's dreams
- to give space for life's unknown surprises
- to connect with the people you treasure
- to tap into your intuition
- to have fun
- to learn something new
- to rejuvenate and relax
- to breathe a little easier
- to get clear about difficult or challenging situations
- to create a more colorful archive of your life

From spiritual practices to carnal pleasures, I have learned that the everyday habits and positive endeavors support us in creating balance, connection, productivity and grounding. The short retreats, whether they are healthy diversions or dreamy virtual experiences, give us a sense of freedom, re-charge the batteries and are fun. Yet, the bigger adventures help us in reaching our pinnacle. Decide what you want to do daily, weekly, monthly and annually. Replace "someday" with today, and start planning an aspiring adventure of a lifetime.

A Coaching Process to Assist in Creating Your Life Adventure:

1. Make a list of things from which you need a break.

2. Now create a list of things you are longing to do.

3. Decide how much time you need for each one… an hour, a day, a week or longer?

4. Choose your first, second and third priorities, and then generate an action item for each of those adventures.

5. Next, craft a stretch goal… what is a getaway activity, dream vacation or immersion that you long for?

6. Finally, take the next step in making your bigger vision a reality.

Ignite Your Inner Passion

July 2008

"What is passion? Passion is surely the becoming of a person."
John Boorman

Do you feel alive and present in your life? Are you doing the things you love in your work, in your home, in your community and your relationships? Are you raising your heart rate on a daily basis, whether you are exercising or making love? Do you have a passion-filled life?

Sometimes when I speak to audiences about passion, people first think of sex or the things they will do some day when they have more time or money. Passion is secondary for many people and so they settle for observing it in books, movies and the lives of others, rather than embracing their own wants, needs and desires. The truth is... passion is a powerful feeling, a strong longing for something or someone, and I believe it needs to be in as many parts of your life as possible.

Passion is the beginning of a dream or an idea. It is the fire burning inside you when you feel completely aligned with your thoughts, feelings, desires and values. Pursuing fervor makes you vulnerable, and encourages you to have ecstatic experiences to give you the confidence and knowingness to start a new path and get what you want. English author Rebecca West said, "It is the soul's duty to be loyal to its own desires. It must abandon itself to its master passion." Passion can be described as a spontaneous act of abandoning all reason and that is exactly what you need to do. Get out of your head, listen to the longing in your heart and intentionally move forward even when it may appear to be irrational, unreasonable and downright crazy.

Excavating your deepest passions are important; you must find ways to outwardly and concretely unleash the suppressed desires that align with who you are and what impact you want to have. The risk of not expressing your essence is the soul's diminishment, a slow death in your relationships from the lack of love and isolation; a deficiency in enthusiasm leading to the waste of your unique talents, the possibility of creating emotional and financial poverty, living with faded dreams and unfilled hopes, and a separation from your Spirit to yourself and God or your Higher Power.

Passion is everywhere, in everything and reflected in everyone. Open your eyes to the passion surrounding you, let it envelope your existence and then tap into your inner knowing of what turns you on. All great ideas start with dedicated excitement, and you must practice fearless fierceness for a passion-filled life. Here are some ideas to turn on your personal passions.

<u>Ways to Turn On Your Passion:</u>

- Be fully present to what you are doing and completely engage with those around you.
- Get out of your head, pay attention to your heart's desires and trust your gut feelings.
- Do things that make you feel good.
- Let your inner beauty be reflected in your outward appearance in your clothes, jewels, hair and make-up.
- Only buy things that you LOVE and have the experiences you WANT.
- Achieve your personal best body for YOU.
- Tap into the five senses of smell, taste, sight, hearing and feeling to create your own sensuality.
- Look for your partner's soul through his/her eyes. Let him or her take your breath away and feel your heart race.
- Make love… A LOT.
- Spend time with people you want to be with, not people you have to—and really get to know them.
- Add romance, magic and sparkle into everything.
- Liberate your physical spaces by cleaning out clutter, bringing in beautiful items and adding colors that inspire whatever emotion you want to feel.
- Go outside and look at the stars.
- Be fierce about your creative pursuits.
- Take time for cultural and art experiences like concerts, art exhibits, lectures, reading and traveling so that you can be inspired.
- Dig in a garden.

- Play with your children.
- Be spontaneous by following your urges.
- Engage in rituals for yourself—prayer, meditation, church, journaling, quiet time, lighting candles and listening to music.
- Eat dark chocolate and drink fine champagne, or anything else in which you take delight.
- Focus on fun, laugh a lot and don't take things too seriously.
- Savor the climatic moments of your life.
- Don't waste another moment… get started NOW.

When you fill your life with divinely-inspired acts, cause no harm and are actively engaged, then your life will transcend and fall into place. Your spiritual, mental, emotional, physical and creative pursuits will attract the perfect partner, the dream job, spiritual connection, the healthy body, the abundant bank account, the completed novel, true friendships and a beautiful home. By playing with possibilities, dreaming about new ventures, meeting zealous people, making a difference for others, and seeing the world from new perspectives, you bring passion not only to yourself but also to those around you. Passion is contagious and available everywhere, in everything and for everyone at any given moment. Ignite your inner passion today.

A Coaching Exercise to Discover, Ignite and Expand Your Personal Passion:

1. By answering the following questions, create a list of the things you are passionate about:

- What activities energize or intoxicate you, get your heart beating faster, take your breath away and make you come alive?
- What makes you HOT and bothered? It might give you some clues as to what you truly care about.
- If making love is bringing love into the world, what can you do to bring more love into the world?

2. Now, give life to your passionate pursuits by sharing this list with your best friend, your partner or coach. Ask him/her to

note when you smile, your energy is higher, your voice picks up and which items make you the happiest.

3. Choose the activities that you were most excited about when you shared your list, prioritize these first and start at least one new passion-filled pursuit today.

Access Your Personal Power

August 2008

"You were born with potential.
You were born with goodness and trust.
You were born with ideals and dreams.
You were born with greatness.
You were born with wings.
You were not meant for crawling, so don't.
You have wings.
Learn to use them and fly."
Rumi

What makes a person powerful? Is it their money, fame, position, charisma, social status or expertise? Some of these things are important, but the most powerful person has the ability to use not only their external resources, but also access and activate their internal gifts and talents. An influential person is first and foremost true to themselves, and their internal make-up is reflected in their outside world of relationships, work, community and environment. Are you using your powers for good?

Powerful people put their stake in the ground on what they know to be their truth and continue moving toward the greater good of self and others. The leadership in their own lives becomes intoxicating to those around them, and they can't help but naturally empower others. Their authentic power is apparent and their intense presence is aligned with their own personal values, continual personal growth and resulting external actions.

Do you feel powerful in your life and if not, why? Maybe you are not tapping into all of your greatest assets or fully using your potential. Perhaps you are still living the "life scripts" someone else gave you or you have forgotten the dreams and aspirations you once had. Maybe you have given your power away to someone who emotionally or financially supports you, but does not truly listen, understand or even know you.

No matter where you are in your life, I believe you can regain your power by taking small steps to access that forgotten energy. After all, your personal power is not something you get from things or others, it is something that already exists within yourself. You just have to remember where it is and then retrieve it.

12 Ways to Access Your Authentic Power:

1. The Power of **Self** Know you and your values, what is important to you and your limitations. Claim your own personal power, as opposed to letting others define you. Identify your own personal power.

2. The Power of **Passion** Know what makes you feel alive and pursue those activities that help you feel connected to yourself, others and your community. What do you care about and what makes you mad in the world? Let that inform you about possible hidden passions.

3. The Power of **Expansion** Dream, visualize, grow and create. The sky is the limit and there are unlimited possibilities and resources.

4. The Power of **Intention** Decide what you want and be fierce for it. Use powerful thoughts, words and actions to support your vision that has meaningful influence and purposeful impact.

5. The Power of **Connection** Share your dreams with others who will hold your ideas and visions. Engage in creative collaboration. Connect to the power sources and the people who feed your soul—loyal advocates, a Higher Power, supportive friends and family.

6. The Power of **Choice** You are always in choice about your thoughts, beliefs, feelings, attitudes and actions. Learn to say no when you mean no and yes when you mean yes. Be real and set appropriate boundaries.

7. The Power of **Words** The permanence of language can be used to motivate, inspire and build up. Or it can be hurtful, harmful

and used to tear down. Listen actively and say what you need to say. Communicate clearly, positively and responsibly.

8. <u>The Power of **Action**</u> A great idea without action is simply an idea. Do something, anything, to make it real. Move, dance, go outside, make a phone call, set up a meeting. Be proactive, not reactive, and get going.

9. <u>The Power of **Risk**</u> Take a chance on changing. Be uncomfortable or unpopular to pursue what you believe to be true. Be bold and fierce. Be afraid and do something anyway.

10. <u>The Power of **Giving**</u> Give your time, talent and resources to others without sacrificing yourself or expecting recognition. Think outside of yourself. Tithe. Be grateful, understanding, kind and compassionate.

11. <u>The Power of **Faith**</u> Let go and trust in God, a Higher Power, or the Universe. Know what you believe in and stand for what is right.

12. <u>The Power of **Wisdom**</u> Trust your intuition, your experiences and your wisdom. Never go against yourself, or cause harm to others.

It is within your power to become as happy, content and successful as you make up your mind to be. Accessing your personal power will create the self-confidence you need to take the necessary actions to ensure your desires come to fruition. By unleashing your power within each of these areas, you can go from feeling powerless to being powerful each and every day.

<u>Powerful Coaching Questions:</u>

1. What is it to be powerful?

2. Who is a powerful role model for you, and what are the qualities in that person that you admire most? What makes them powerful?

3. Of these admirable qualities and referencing the above list, what do you already possess that will make you more able to reach your full vitality?

4. Are there any people, circumstances or beliefs to which you give your power away? To whom, when and under what circumstances? If so, how can you change course?

5. Do you speak powerfully with influence, grace and integrity in order to respect the people you come in contact with on a daily basis?

6. Are you being a powerful leader by inspiring, teaching, influencing, modeling or mentoring others?

7. Do you recognize the number of powerful, authentic choices you have each and every day?

8. Using the list above, create the Inspired Actions you will take to expand your own power base.

Don't Settle for Being Second

September 2008

> "It's a funny thing about life. If you refuse to settle for anything less than the best, that's what it will give you."
> Somerset Maugham

In considering this month's theme, the #2 issue, I started to think about how many times people settle for being second, as opposed to truly embracing being first. Two is a great number for partnerships, but when it comes to having authentic, fulfilling relationships, how often do you or others you know settle for being the consolation prize?

It is interesting to me that people can accomplish much in many areas of their lives, yet when it comes to their relationships or their careers, they often resolve themselves or make compromises that do not honor what they truly need and desire. It seems like when the emotional stakes are at their highest, the bargaining begins. Stories get created such as someone, somehow, someday "it" will change and hope, coupled with denial, sets in. People hang on to promises made and they accept that their current career, life situation or relationship is as good as it gets. Even worse, some people do not even believe they deserve a better job, a wonderful relationship or the abundance that goes with a happy life. So, they settle for less without ever considering what they really need, much less speaking up for it.

Being first means knowing yourself, doing your best and asking for what you want. It starts with being clear about your needs, being proactive in achieving your dreams, and getting fierce for your desires. Making yourself a priority means asking people to assist you and if they are not able to, finding someone who can. Insist on congruency with others in their words and actions and expect them to put you at the top of the list. Demand respect and start being treasured by the people closet to you for who you truly are, as well as your gifts, talents and personal excellence. And above all, get your needs met and be at the top of your own list.

Identifying Your Needs:

Getting needs met can be a tricky thing. As humans, we have wants and desires, but often don't properly identify what's really missing or needed. In order to start living more authentically and joyfully, you must name it, claim it and take action. Consider what "needs" you currently have **relationally, emotionally, spiritually, financially and physically.** Listed below are the more prevalent needs I have observed in my coaching practice.

Some Common Needs:
> *To be valued, recognized, validated*
> *To be appreciated*
> *To be loved, cherished, adored, treasured, supported, approved of, acknowledged, cared for, accepted unconditionally, saved, rescued*
> *To be included, to belong, to feel part of*
> *To be liked*
> *To be certain, sure, confident, positive*
> *To be comfortable, nurtured*
> *To be free, independent, self-reliant*
> *To be noticed, remembered, seen*
> *To be of service, a leader, a follower*
> *To be trusted*
> *To be heard, listened to*
> *To feel important, needed, useful, busy*
> *To feel connected (to others, to a Higher Power, to yourself)*
> *To feel safe, secure, protected, stable*
> *To have beauty, order, consistency, perfection*
> *To have peace, calm, quiet, stillness, balance*
> *To have power, strength, influence, acclaim, control*
> *To have abundance, security, stability*
> *To have a cause, vocation, higher purpose*
> *To have honesty, sincerity, loyalty, authenticity, integrity*
> *To have fun, laughter, joy*
> *To have passion, play, pleasure*
> *To have companionship*
> *To have physical touch, connection*

An Exercise in Discovering How To Get Your Needs Met:

1. What would your life look if you were number one?

2. What's missing in your life that keeps you from experiencing true fulfillment and joy in your work and your relationships? Are there boundaries or requests you need to make?

3. Using the above list, identify the three most important "needs" you currently want fulfilled, then rank them in order of importance to you.

4. Design three creative ways to meet each need.

5. Take responsibility to meet your own needs AND enlist four different people to meet each need for the next month—be sure to include yourself. Overdo it! Here are some examples:

   - If you need to feel approval or validation, you might ask your boss for weekly check-in meetings or to tell you when you do a good job.
   - If you need to feel adored, you might ask your partner to tell you how fabulous you are and maybe what qualities he or she likes about you.
   - If you needed to feel peaceful, you might schedule daily quiet time, start a meditation practice or go for a walk, without technology.
   - If you need to feel accomplishment, you might make a list of your achievements you have done this year, so far.

6. You might consider having your best friend, boss or partner also do this exercise and then compare notes.

(See "Excavating Your Needs" coaching exercise in the Appendix.)

Be Who You Are

October 2008

> "By being yourself, you put something wonderful in the world
> that was not there before."
> Edwin Elliot

Do you know who you really are, or do you hide behind a façade of selected masks and prescribed roles that have been handed to you by others? Do you reveal what is really important to you in the world, or simply shrink low when it is your turn to speak? Society regularly asks us to fit in and to follow the norms, but does it void your vibrancy and suppress your spirit? If so, you are not alone.

Knowing who you are is important if you want to discover the full expression of yourself, and to experience deep love, peaceful freedom and essential authenticity. Being real is created by aligning your internal and external worlds with your thoughts and actions. Creating new ways of being in the world apart from your chosen roles takes time and courage. It requires a willingness to face fear, look deep inside and examine learned behaviors or bad habits. Only then can you experience being fully who you are not only with others, but also with the most important person: you.

12 Ways to Excavate Yourself:

1. **Live Your Values**- Identify your values, what is important to you, and how you want to live in this world. Claim who you are, as opposed to letting others define you. Think about how you can live your life in alignment with your values. What are some of the values you have as an individual? What is really important to you? Name eight to ten values. (See "A Sampling of Traditional Values" in the Appendix.)

2. **Embrace Beauty**- People often say that beauty lies in the eye of the beholder. That means you get to hold the power over what you believe is beautiful to you, inside and out. Are you acquainted with what is gorgeous to YOU and what stirs your senses? Notice appealing sights, smells, textures, shapes, and forms. Beauty is an inside job, so discover your own personal style and then let it reflect everywhere... in your clothes, home, music, art, nature, work you create. Define what beauty means to you by creating a collage or vision board of the things you love, desire and want.

3. **Pursue Passion**- Know, what makes you feel alive and consciously follow those activities that help you feel connected to yourself and others. Dance, sing, play, travel, dream, visualize, grow and create. Seek and expand your possibilities. What makes you feel alive? List five passions.

4. **Love What You Do**- Are you following your bliss? Is your work irresistible, meaningful, or important to you? Engage in something you adore and brings you joy on a daily basis, even if it looks messy or unexplainable to others. Be fierce for it. Do you love what you do? If so, great. If not, list your top ten dream jobs and then take one step each day to move towards the one that is most compelling.

5. **Be in Choice**- You are always free to choose your thoughts, beliefs, attitudes and actions. Learn to say NO when you mean no, and yes when you mean YES. What do you choose in any given moment...heavy or light; easy or hard? Are you consciously making your choices with your thoughts, words, and actions? Create a "Yes, No and Maybe" list. Decide who and what you will say yes to, and who and what you will say no to. (See "Yes, No and Maybe List" coaching exercise in the Appendix.)

6. **Practice Gratitude**- Be thankful, understanding, kind, and compassionate; express it often. Let people know how much you appreciate them and what they do. Who and what are you grateful for? Start a Gratitude journal, say prayers of thanks, and acknowledge others' generous acts. List 25 things for which you are grateful. (See "Excavating Your Gratitude" coaching exercise in the Appendix.)

7. **Ask for What You Want**- Do you know what you REALLY, REALLY, REALLY want? Practice wanting. If you ask for what you desire, you just might get it. Not asking is an automatic no. Communicate clearly and positively. And, besides, who knows what you want and need better than you? What do you want? Make a list of your deepest desires, both actual items and intangible wants.

8. **Trust Yourself**- Trust your intuition. Your experiences will inform you, as well as your faith and wisdom to never go against yourself. Develop your self-confidence. Do you trust yourself? Upon whose opinion are you seeking or depending? Create a daily practice of peace, quiet and stillness, and then ask yourself the same questions you ask others.

9. **Clear Clutter**- What are you holding on to? People, places and things? Old memories, piles of stuff in your home or office? How are these "things" holding you captive? Keeping the unneeded holds an energy that will often hold you back, so clean it out. NOW. What people, places and things are you holding on to? Decide what will you get rid of today, and do it now.

10. **Have Playmates**- Are you spending time with people who honor you, celebrate you, or have similar interests, goals, values and vision? Engage in creative collaboration and amazing alliances. Who can you get to play with you on a project? Don't go it alone. Find people with whom you have fun personally and professionally. Enrich your circle

of connection and enlarge your playgrounds. Choose your playmates and then connect with <u>at least</u> one person you care about each day.

11. **Try It Anyway**- What holds you back? Is it a belief, an old story, low self-esteem or simply a bad habit? Risk changing. Be afraid. Do it anyway. A great idea without action is simply an idea, so do something new or different that moves you towards living your rich, authentic, rewarding life. Make a list of all of your fears and then put it away. Next, do the ONE thing you think you can not do, try it and you will be amazed at what you learn about yourself.

12. **Celebrate Success**- When you reach your goals, do you stop to enjoy your fruits? Do you acknowledge your hard work, perseverance and determination? Rejoice and revel in all that you do and have done. Learn to savor. How will you celebrate, with whom and when? Create an Accomplishment List of the things you have done over the past year so you can see how far you have come. Add to it and embrace your fabulousness. (See "Excavating Your Accomplishments" coaching exercise in the Appendix.)

A Revealing Exercise to Help You Take the Mask Off and Be Your Best Self:

Take a blank piece of paper. On one side, write "MY PORTRAYED SELF" This is the person you show to the outside world, the many roles you play. On the other side, write "MY REAL SELF" and describe the qualities and values you believe you hold, in other words, your true essences.

Next, find a trusted person to share what you uncover about yourself—your secrets, fears, insecurities as well as dreams, desires and plans. Observe what is different on each side, and then brainstorm some ways to bring these two different sides into alignment.

Time Is On Your Side

November 2008

> "All great achievements require time."
> Maya Angelou

Do you have enough time? Are you always trying to manage your schedule so you can squeeze a little more juice out of the few extra minutes and hours in a day? Do you feel like your schedule is driven by the demands of others, or worse, unrealistic expectations you hold for yourself? Do you have the need to know all of the answers NOW?

In thinking about writing this column about time, I considered sharing with you time management techniques, yet I decided organization is only part of the problem. As a Life Coach, I often hear about my clients' frustrations over not having enough moments to do the things they really want to do because they have so many other obligations and demands. They are in a hurry to do more, be more, achieve more. They have fewer occasions to do it and they engage in more distractions than ever. They want to find the answers quickly to resolve problems, to understand each other and to know outcomes; yet, many people do not understand how time can work for them, not against them. Does this sound like you?

I focus on helping people understand that time really is on their side. Hours can not be added to your day, but you can make better choices on how to use time and see it as an asset. By accepting a more natural flow to your life, learning to prioritize what is most important to you and being patient with the outcomes, you can learn to trust in the rhythm of nature and discover that there is perfect timing in all areas of your life.

Time is on your side, so breathe and relax into your life. Discover what is most essential to you and then use your time to create more peace and harmony, more space to do the things you really want and more connection to the people you love and care about. Here are some suggestions for developing a new way to honor and manage your time...

Four Timely Habits to Instill into Your Routine:

1. **Create "Real-time" Expectations-** Be realistic and learn to break down greater undertakings into smaller increments. Don't delay starting projects because you think you need a large block of time. Expectations and worrying about how much time something will take can eat up a large chunk of your day or even week. Every year I fret about gathering my tax information, thinking it will take many hours to compile, when in actuality, it only takes a couple of hours. So, get started and just do the tasks, one step at a time. Exercise to try- Take a task or chore and devote only 15 minutes per day to it, no more, and see how much you can accomplish. Review your cumulative progress in a week or month.

2. **Trust Your Internal Clock-** Listen to your own intuition and be in charge of your time. Stop letting your watch drive you, and relearn how to let life flow naturally and easily. Not having electricity for several days after a storm outage allowed me to reset my body clock. I went to bed when it was dark and arose when the sun came out, and I felt extremely rested. Trust that you will know what to do and when to do it. Exercise to try- Give up your watch for the day and trust your internal clock to get you wherever you need to be. Start on the weekend if that is easier.

3. **Develop Discernment with Your Time-** What is it you are REALLY trying to accomplish? Are you doing the things you want to do, or are you following a long list of things you think you should be doing? Be wise with your time and consider who you give your time to and for what reasons. I allow laundry to pile up if it means I can spend time with a friend. Exercise to try- Create a "Yes, No and Maybe" list. Decide who and what you will say yes, and to who and what you will say no. (See "Yes, No & Maybe List" coaching exercise in the Appendix.)

4. **<u>Understand Divine Timing</u>**- Over time, the missing piece of the puzzle or the right person will always be revealed. If you push for something when the timing is not right, then you might miss out on something better than what you had wanted in the first place. Practice patience and allow for everything to work out perfectly. My business grew when I was ready to accept the responsibility. Exercise to try- Create a "God Box." Write down your questions and put these into a special container and let go of the stressful thoughts. Allow God, the Universe or your particular belief system to take over. You can refer back to it after a designated period of time to see if anything has been revealed to you.

American writer Carl Sandberg said, "Time is a great teacher." Don't miss the opportunity to learn the important life lessons, and let each moment in time be part of your growth, reflection and inspiration. Time is on your side, so start making the most of it today.

<u>Coaching Questions to Reclaim Your Time:</u>

1. What would you do with more time?

2. With whom do you spend your time? Do they give you energy or take it away?

3. Is your deadline real, or did you make it up? Or is there something on your list that can be moved to another day?

4. Describe your perfect day, week or month.

Let Your Inner Light Shine

December 2008

> "Let nothing dim the light that shines from within."
> Maya Angelou

When I started thinking about what is sparkly, bright and shiny, I considered all things glittery… flickering lights, dazzling jewels, shimmering stars, sunlit landscapes, disco balls on a dance floor, the twinkle of an eye. Light enables us to see clearly, and when objects are lit, they become alive and fully illuminated to a greater state of being.

The same thing happens to people. When a person sparkles, it is because they let their inner light shine. I love seeing the look on one's face when he or she is filled with love, joy and happiness. The way a person carries themselves, the tone of their voice and the look in their eyes are great indicators of how fulfilled a person truly is. I often wonder where sparkle comes from. What creates radiance, and how can one use their brilliance to be genuine with themselves and the world?

When I am coaching my clients, I search for ways to assist them in excavating their beauty and authenticity and how to integrate that into their lives. After clarifying their values, goals, dreams and desires, I often use a diamond as a metaphor in life to help them see that they are a rough diamond and can create greater value. Just as a diamond cutter finds the perfect shape to honor the stone he holds, my clients must find the many facets of their own magnificence and polish them to capture the perfect light so they can sparkle and shine brightly.

Brilliance is difficult to describe, yet you recognize it when you see it. It is a bright idea, a quiet resolve, a passionate performance, an ingenious insight, a soaring aspiration, a bold choice or a compassionate act. A person's brilliance comes from within, putting courageous self-trust into action. When you learn to embrace the many aspects of yourself, you can claim who you are and then positively impact the world around you.

Polish the Four C's of Life:

Diamonds are a girl's best friend, especially when you learn that YOU could be the biggest, best and most brilliant diamond you own. Start with the "Four C's" to increase your own value and self-worth.

1. **CUT** Remove the clutter in your life. Clean up the redundancy and trite ways of seeing how dreary life can be. Remove the opaqueness and negativity, so that you start polishing up your life.

2. **CLARITY** Be clear about who you are, your values and your life's vision. Your resources, whether they are time, talent or money, can be put to greater use once you have clear intentions as to what you want your life to be about.

3. **COLOR** Take action to live fully, creating depth and meaning in all you do. It is the passionate experiences, spiritual connection and playful encounters that put the color in your life.

4. **CARAT** Increase your carat weight through the fulfillment of your dreams, giving you limitless possibilities. Live with gratitude and learn how to be of service to yourself and to others. The more multi-dimensional facets you claim, the more weight and value you will have.

Spiritual leader and author Marianne Williamson has been inspiring people all over the world with a quote from her book *A Return to Love*. "Our deepest fear is not that we are inadequate. Our deepest fear is that we are powerful beyond measure. It is our light, not our darkness, that most frightens us. We ask ourselves, who am I to be brilliant, gorgeous, talented and fabulous? Actually, who are you *not* to be? You are a child of God. Your playing small does not serve the world. There is nothing enlightened about shrinking so that other people won't feel insecure around you. We are all meant to shine, as children do. We were born to make manifest the glory of God that is within us. It's not just in some of us; it's in everyone. And as we let our own light shine, we unconsciously give other people permission to do the same. As we are liberated from our own fear, our presence automatically liberates others."

I challenge you to think about the unique qualities you have and how they stand out in the world. Give yourself permission to shine so that you can positively impact anyone and everyone around you. Be a model to others and sparkle everywhere you go.

<u>Coaching Questions to Help Your Light Shine:</u>

1. List your gifts and talents. Think about how these show up in the many areas of your life and how you want to share them with others.

2. What is ONE thing you always think of that makes you smile?

3. What facets of your life do you need to polish or clean up?

4. Do you live from the inside out, or outside in?

5. Describe how you are "brilliant, gorgeous, talented and fabulous."

(See "Excavive™ Permission Slip" in the Appendix.)

Have Hope and Take Inspired Action

January 2009

"Once you choose hope, anything's possible."
Christopher Reeve

Most people get inspired to set new goals and make positive changes at the beginning of a new year... but I wonder why wait until a predetermined, traditional time of year to set new intentions and take steps toward achieving your wishes. If you are ready to make a change in any area of your life, a fresh start can happen at anytime. Whether you are restless, inspired, discouraged, have had setbacks and challenges or simply feel the need to begin again, why wait until you are struggling or are forced to take action? Regardless of your current circumstances, have you given thought to and revisited your hopes, dreams and desires much less done something about it?

Maybe you have your own personal challenges of a job loss, failing health, a dying relationship or, perhaps you are questioning your own ability to be strong enough for what could be in front of you. It can be easy to get discouraged and do nothing. I find that people can easily lose faith, and often do not have the tools, supporters or clear vision to move past their hopelessness. Change can be scary, even paralyzing, until the pain of suffering outweighs the fear of the unknown, and then forward movement can start to occur.

What keeps you going when it seems like there is no hope? How do you find the strength to persevere, the energy to do something positive and the drive to reach for your dreams when things appear to be falling apart, or even worse, seem to be downright hopeless?

In challenging, fearful or unfulfilled times, having hope and taking action are not only a winning combination but also essential in manifesting your fullest life. After all, how can you move forward if you do not at least start with hope? Hope is the belief in and desire for something better than the present. You cannot be positive without a faithful belief that all will work out; that good wins over evil; that there is an innate goodness in all things. This optimism can give you the feeling what you want can be achieved and the outcomes to life's challenges, events and circumstances can ultimately be conquered with positive results.

Life coaching begins with hope but the process quickly moves people into action. There is a foundational belief that people are "creative, resourceful and whole and they have the answers within themselves," [1] and this sets the tone for self-empowerment. My clients do not need to be "fixed," yet they often need to take bolder, more assertive steps to break bad habits, eliminate fears and create momentum. By tapping into integrated values, claiming realistic goals or intentions, and creating enthused actions, they gain the tools to have relentless courage and the self-confidence to have a great life.

Hope is essential, but it's not enough by itself. Hope needs to be coupled with enthused deeds to turn a life vision into everyday reality so nice thoughts do not end up as simply beautiful dreams, a grown-up fairy tale or an on-going illusion. Even "hinting and hoping" (the way one wants something and wishes to get it without ever asking for it or doing something concrete about it) and "visualizing and manifesting" are not sole methods to making things happen. You must also take action derived from inspiration. So use the positive energy created from hope, combine it with authentic goals and take inspired action to create everything you want for an enthusiastically blissful life.

12 Questions to Create Inspired Action:

In answering the following questions, you might consider how your answers apply in eight major life areas: Career & Education; Money;

---

1   Whitworth, Laura; Kimsey-House, Henry; Sandahl; Co-Active Coaching, Mountain View, Davies-Black Publishing

Health & Wellness; Friends & Family; Romantic Relationship; Personal Growth & Spirituality; Fun & Play; and Physical Spaces.

1. What have you learned about yourself and your values, your accomplishments and your failures in the past year?

2. What do you hope for now and beyond?

3. Starting NOW, what if the rest of your life was the best of your life?

4. Do you know how to dream with your eyes wide open? If what's in your dreams wasn't already inside of you, how could you even dream it?

5. What is your unrelenting passion?

6. Why this goal, or these goals?

7. Are your goals great and compelling or vague and uninspiring?

8. How far would you go to chase what you really want?

9. Where does adventure live for you?

10. If not you, who? If not now, when?

11. Are you taking concrete steps to manifest your reality?

12. Have you begun today what you wish for tomorrow?

Make a list of your answers. Next, generate any related actions that inspire you. (See "Inspired Action Items" coaching exercise in the Appendix.)

When you begin to take specific steps towards what you want, you can synergize a cumulative effect on other areas of your life as well. For example, when you start working out, it makes you not only look good, but feel better. You then smile more, are at ease, are nicer and attract people who want to be with you. You then become more motivated in your work, do a better job, get a promotion or raise, etc.

So, envision a new beginning by expanding your hopes and dreams, moving forward with inspired actions and embracing the rest of your wonderful life. Drew Rozell Ph.D. said, "So I need to create a vision of what I want that will bring all of my intentions together. And a vision is just that—something I can see, something that's so exciting and attractive to me that it pulls me forward until I have it." Have hope, open up to limitless possibilities and discover what awaits you in the world.

Ah, Love, Sweet Love: The Sweetness of Romantic Love

February 2009

> "Life has taught us that love does not consist in gazing at each other
> but in looking outward together in the same direction."
> Antoine de Saint-Exupéry

In giving consideration to this month's sugar theme, many things came to mind and I kept asking myself, what makes life so sweet? I considered a discussion on defining, creating, balancing and maintaining the many aspects of a sweet life. However, when I got to the heart of what I wanted to share, love emerged... not just the universal, spiritual, higher consciousness, greater love for all mankind and the various relationships that make up our world, but truly, deeply, madly romantic love and the criteria needed to sustain a healthy relationship. After all, when it comes down to what people want most in life, isn't it just to love and be loved?

So, what is love? How do you know you are in love? And, why do so many people invest so much of themselves in looking for love? In her book *Finding True Love*, Daphne Rose Kingma defined love as "an experience of great emotional and spiritual awakening to the unbounded bliss that is the true condition of our souls. When we fall in love, we feel no separation between ourselves and the person we love or, for a time, from all others. It is the transcendent, luminous, lovely feeling of love that we desire most dearly, long for most passionately, and are filled by most deeply when it occurs in our lives. Love is a sanctuary for our spirits, a bath of empathy for our emotions, a tranquil meadow in which to nurture our fond hopes and dreams." Love makes us feel good, alive and purposeful, whether you are in a relationship, looking for one or choosing to be alone.

It is important to understand some basics to having amorous love, and it includes self-love, loving the other person and loving the relationship itself. Nourish and love yourself first and always be who you are; say what you feel and ask for what you need courageously; cherish your mate unconditionally; continually practice compassion and forgiveness; align your words and actions; treasure your relationship by celebrating, playing, remembering and honoring it; and show your love by making sure your words and actions match. Finally, practice three vital tools to sustain and grow your love… communicate consistently, co-create it by having a shared vision and deepen it with the passion that exists.

My Top Three Tools for Sustaining Love in a Romantic Relationship:

1. **Communication** is essential for a successful relationship. Many relationships suffer from poor or little communication skills, so you need to gain the tools needed to share your feelings and to ask for what you need. Realize your partner's needs may not match yours, so talk about them. Disclose your thoughts, dreams, fears, hopes, wants, desires, opinions and anything else that comes to mind. Revealing your inner self creates intimacy, a deep bonding and a lasting connection. In *The Five Love Languages* developed by Gary Chapman, he identified the ways in which people feel loved: Physical Touch, Words of Affirmation, Quality Time, Acts of Service and Gifts. Do you know how you feel most loved, and what about your partner?

2. **Shared Vision** is about co-creating a life together. Do you know what direction you want to go, and does your partner want to go with you? For example, do you both want children? Do you prefer to create a quiet life at home, or would you rather see the world together? Identifying your common interests and what goals you want to work toward will keep your relationship fresh, purposeful and on the same path.

3. **Passion** in romance sets apart your relationship from all others. What is it to love deeply and from the heart? When we have chemistry, a desire for our partner and the sexual expression of that, it creates a deeper connection and bond with the other person. What is pleasure? Learn about each other, be generous,

take delight in each other's bodies—find the fervor, the zeal. It is easy to let the flame burn out way too soon in a relationship, so discover ways to keep the fire burning.

A Coaching Exercise to Enrich Your Romantic Relationship:

Are you the type of person with whom you would to spend the rest of your life? If so, you are ready for lasting love. An exercise I use with my Life Coaching clients when we work on their romantic relationship is a Wheel of Relationship that examines the level of happiness and satisfaction in 12 major areas of their partnership. This process provides perspective, balance and focus on what is working and what might need attention. If you were at your best, what would you do in your relationship right now? (See the "Wheel of Relationships" coaching exercise in the Appendix.)

In each of these twelve areas, rate your level of joy and satisfaction on a scale of 1-10:

1. Shared Goals/Vision & Creativity

2. Communication & Conflict Resolution

3. Love, Emotional Health & Happiness

4. Career

5. Money

6. Sexual Expression & Physical Intimacy

7. Family

8. Celebrations, Rituals & Gifts

9. Social Life & Friends

10. Spirituality & Sacred Time

11. Fun & Play

12. Physical Spaces

To keep love alive and your relationship sweet, go for the kind, pure, raw, true, blissful, real love. Not the kind that is artificial or manufactured, but rather the kind that is natural and has its flaws, but is always authentic and sweet to the taste. In doing so, love can not only satisfy your soul, but also lead you back to your most authentic self. In this higher purpose, you can then reach your greatest potential and spread love to the rest of the world. Savor it, appreciate it, honor it and respect it... ah, love, sweet love.

Go with the Flow

March 2009

> "Nature often holds up a mirror so we can see more clearly the ongoing processes of growth, renewal and transformation in our lives."
> Mary Ann Bussat

Do you experience ease and flow in your life? Are you at peace with where your life is, or do you constantly worry, try to force the answers or attempt to control everything that comes your way? Do you enjoy the rhythm of your life, or are you stressed out, worried, anxious and constantly on the go, even when you don't have to be?

Understanding your own natural rhythm, as well as the natural order of life, can bring not only more peaceful fluidity, but also moments of ecstasy and joy. Highs and lows convey recognition of what works, what does not work and how to choose more discerning life solutions. Consider the ups and downs of your life path—I suspect there have been happy, peak experiences as well as lonely, confusing disappointments.

No one is immune to difficult circumstances such as a personal illness, a paralyzing ice storm, a financial setback, the ending of a relationship, a difficult co-worker or the deceit of another. But it is in those challenging moments when there are transformational opportunities to trust, evolve and come back even stronger than before.

Aviator and author Anne Morrow Lindbergh wrote, "We have so little faith in the ebb and flow of life, of love, of relationships. We leap at the flow of the tide and resist in terror at its ebb. We are afraid it will never return. We insist on permanency, on duration, on continuity; when the only continuity possible, in life as in love, is in growth, in fluidity- in freedom, in the sense that the dancers are free, barely touching as they pass, but partners in the same pattern."

Where does faith and freedom play a role in your life? Find your personal liberty by trusting yourself, following your creative energies, listening to your body and surrounding yourself with advocates. Find a higher faith that will sustain, ground and instill hope that all will be well and work out in the end of the roller coaster ride of life.

That life continues to happen and change is a certainty, so I encourage you to stop attempting to disrupt the natural flow of your life. A coaching exercise I use involves examining beliefs to see if they are empowering and can move you forward, or are limiting and holding you back. By becoming aware of where you might be stuck, you can start actively pursuing your own energetic flows to create more aliveness, connectivity, creativity and passion.

Thoughts that Keep You from "Being in the FLOW"—And How to Turn Them Around:

Limiting Beliefs to Release:	Empowering Thoughts to Embrace:
TURN….	INTO…
Fear	Trusting love
Prescriptive expectations	Possibilities & openness
Perfection	Balance & boundaries
Controlling behaviors	Relinquishing outcomes
Limiting beliefs	Inspired actions
Mediocrity	Mastery
Distracted clutter	Beauty
Judgment of self & others	Full acceptance
Self-consciousness	Vulnerably dropping the mask
Self-centeredness	Compassionate connections
Headstrong reasoning	Fierce intuition
Drama	Peaceful purpose & direction
Anger	Motivating passion
Caring what others think	Detachment
Making assumptions	Clear communications
Regrets	Positively trying again
Guilt & shame	Endless gratitude & respect
Failure	Learning opportunities
Doing it alone	Creative collaboration
Powerlessness	Powerful choices

Don't allow the spinning tales, made-up stories and unfounded fears hold you hostage in your life. Become consciously aware and be truthful about what is disrupting your life flow. Only then can you seek good intentions from the ebb and flow of what is given to you each and every day.

Coaching Questions to Create Flow and Fluidity in Your Life:

1. What is creating your reality today, and how is your fear paralyzing you? List EVERYTHING that scares you and ask yourself if it is really true or not.

2. How have you withheld yourself from life?

3. From the above list, choose your biggest limiting belief; think about your behaviors associated with it and then consider the results. To turn it around, work backward by asking, what is the desired result, the desired behavior and then create a new empowering principle.

4. Do you often choose to do things the hard way, or find ways to make everything easy, light or playful?

5. What would a fluid life look like? Create your possibilities of a flowing vision for a day, a week, a month and a year.

The Value in Vintage

April 2009

"It is never too late to be what you might have been."
George Eliot

Why do we like "vintage" so much? Is it the novelty of owning something that has a past, perhaps a great story or memory? Does it provide a personal memento that keeps us connected to a sweeter time, another love, a meaningful relative? Does the craftsmanship represent something of quality and beauty that is no longer made in the same way?

When I think of vintage, several things come to mind… the rich flavor of a great wine; the fine lines of a well-designed car; the perfect taste of an aged cheese; the beauty of classic designer clothing; the craftsmanship of antique furniture; the detail of a well-built older home. *Vintage* creates value in our things: how does that apply to people, our relationships and what is really significant in our lives? Have YOU become better over time?

It seems to me that the problem with people, and our current world situation, is that they have forgotten who they are and what is important to them. They have traded quality for quantity, disposed of anything or anyone who no longer suited their needs and "the bigger the better" became their fighting cry. Flash, glitz and ostentatiousness became the goal rather appreciating what they are already have. The focus for many has been the acquisition of the right car or home, the building of a larger portfolio, sculpting the perfect body and belonging to the right social circles. In the process, many have become not only personally bankrupt, but even worse, spiritually disconnected from themselves and starved for love and connection to others.

Remembering where you came from, learning from your past experiences and reclaiming your essence will assist you in being your best. When you re-instill qualities such as knowing your values, spending quality time with yourself, seeking wisdom from your elders, staying in integrity with your words and actions, doing meaningful work, pursuing your deepest passions and getting to know others based on personality, ethical beliefs and depth of character, then you can begin to take bold authentic actions to recalibrate a more meaningful life. Here are some tips on assessing your own history so you can craft an empowering life story.

12 Tips for Valuing Your Past:

1. **Honor your past experiences** with reverence for what was beautiful and good: capture the fine memories by storytelling, journals, photos, videos and celebrations.

2. **Explore your heritage.** Studying your past, your family's ancestors and your cultural connections may teach you something new about yourself.

3. **Seek wisdom** from the elders in our world, those who have gone before you.

4. **Let history inform you** by learning from your mistakes and becoming a wiser steward of your soul.

5. **Tell the truth.** Are you telling the truth or creating a better story than what perhaps existed?

6. **Don't stay stuck** in your illusionary stories or harmful anger. If you do, seek help from a professional therapist or coach.

7. **Let go** of the unneeded old to make room for the desired new. Find the balance.

8. **Forgive,** but don't forget.

9. **Expect chivalrous gestures.** You deserve respect. Good old-fashioned manners still matter. (After all, I am a southern Texas girl.)

10. **Remember the important people from your past.** Let them know you care—any day is good day to express gratitude, not just birthdays or anniversaries.

11. **Create rituals** that generate your life's archive and continue to bring you back to your core.

12. **Be fierce for you.** Reclaim and remember your essence.

A Coaching Exercise to Assist You in Reconnecting to Who You Are:

1. Think about your spouse, family members, friends, teachers, coaches, bosses or spiritual leaders who have mentored you, taken a positive interest in you, molded your strong morals, ethics or other qualities. Write a gratitude letter to them, sharing the character traits you admire most in them.

2. Next, write a similar letter to yourself, expressing the same individuality, consistent values, or other positive attributes that you recognized in others and believe you also have, or strive to have, in your life.

3. Finally, using the prevalent themes above, complete these sentences: "I was born at this time in history in order to ___" and "I plan to take ___ actions to live up to my best version of me."

When you begin to take specific steps toward remembering who you really are, including your rich history and experiences, and creating a perspective that includes all of you, you will begin to live a more complete life, and will no longer settle for mediocrity, materialism or inauthenticity. The value in vintage is in bringing you back to your true self—what better gift to give the world than the true, lovable, fantastic you.

Connect to Your Sexual Self

May 2009

> "The fiery moments of a passionate experience are moments of
> wholeness and totality."
> Anais Nin

Do you feel satisfied and connected to your sexual self? Are you bonding with your partner in a deeply intimate physical way? Do you have a passion-filled life that includes connection, creativity, self-nurturer and love? Are you getting your sexual needs met on a regular basis, whether you are with or without a partner? Sex is important—AND let me say upfront… it is not my job to judge, regulate or put rules around morality—that is up to you and your belief system. However, as a Life Coach, I assist others in discovering how to achieve the most fulfilling life possible while maintaining equilibrium. When thinking about life balance, the physical, sexual and sensual needs are part of that formula as well.

As humans, physical intimacy is not only needed but also critical for survival. The need to be touched, caressed and desired is real, and it is essential to be aware of the sexual part of yourself that is good, natural and powerful. Your sensuality is given the chance to come alive when you are in your body while allowing your emotions to be present. By understanding this part of yourself, you can tap into your own passions and desires as well as channel your sexual energy—whether it's having sex to deepen the connection with your partner; to procreate and have children; or to give birth to a new way of living or a creative project.

Being in charge of your sexual self gives you freedom and independence, especially when you realize you are in control of your decisions and what is right for you. Most pleasure for women takes place above the waist, as we are highly emotional creatures, so it is important to be intellectually turned on. Physical cravings are often dictated by factors such as body image, mental and emotional stability, safety and trust in your partner, balanced hormones, a stress-free life and fulfillment in other existing areas. Making healthy choices not only creates physical pleasure and passion, but is also a form of empowerment, self-expression, imagination, and, more importantly, can deepen the spiritual intimacy with your partner and yourself.

One of the biggest problems I have observed regarding sex revolves around a person's self-worth. Too many times, I see people who give their power away sexually by not expressing their true desires. They don't have the confidence to ask for what they really want, compromise themselves to keep a relationship that is not right for them rather than be alone, have completely shut down their sexual selves, or use sex to feel validated, powerful or self-important.

Perhaps past messages about sex such as "sex is bad," "good girls don't enjoy sex" or "having sex before marriage or outside a committed relationship is sleazy" add to the lack of worth. However, recreating a strong self-esteem will give you sexual freedom and allow your passion to easily flow.

Here Are Some Ways to Rebuild a Robust Sexual Self-Esteem:

- Understand what you really want and desire both sexually and in other areas of life.
- Discover as many of your passions as possible.
- Deepen your understanding of your sensual self by tapping into your five senses of smell, taste, sight, hearing and feeling.
- Choose a healthy lifestyle in order to be your physical best.
- Make eye contact, smile and exude confidence.
- Build a safe and trusting relationship where sex can flourish.
- Learn what you do not know and are curious about.
- Become an expert at saying no and creating boundaries.
- Express yourself with powerful communication skills and actions.
- Foster self-confidence by feeling as good about your inner self as you do your outer self.
- Follow your urges, and be playfully spontaneous. Make love OFTEN.
- Strengthen your spiritual connection.
- Value a richly purposeful life, with or without a partner.

You have the right to a fantastic sex life. If you are currently satisfied, keep the flames burning. If not, and you desire sexual happiness, regain your sexual confidence by putting the focus on yourself first. Sex can be an area that can either build you up or break you down… get to know your sensual self and the empowerment that exists within you.

Questions to Provoke Thought About Your Sensual and Sexual Self:

1. By answering the following questions, you can learn more about your sensual self and sexual needs:

• Are you satisfied with your sex life? Your partner? What is the distinction between feeling good and being fulfilled both sexually and generally?
• Are you using sex to feel better about yourself and build a false sense of security; or to be expressive and create a connection?
• What are your beliefs about sex? What messages were you given while growing up that may no longer serve you?
• Are your actions authentic by aligning with your values and who you really are? Are they life affirming or life numbing?
• Create your own definition of sexual integrity.
• Do you withhold yourself or settle for less in not only your sexual life but life in general? How?
• Who are your favorite bewitching men/women, and what qualities do they possess that you could emanate?

2. Now, "right-size" sex in your life. In other words, assess where you are now, decide what you need, determine what's normal for you and give yourself permission to ask for what you want from yourself and your partner.

3. Choose three strategies that will strengthen your sexual self-esteem and start implementing those today.

Unplug

June 2009

> "Some people have a wonderful capacity to appreciate again and again, freshly and naively, the basic goods of life, with awe, pleasure, wonder, and even ecstasy."
> Abraham H. Maslow

When I first considered this month's "lazy" theme, I wanted to make a case for inspiring people to get motivated, overcoming procrastination, taking action to create a better life and getting started NOW. One of the reasons people hire a Life Coach is to hold them accountable to take concrete action-oriented steps to move towards their goals and dreams. In a fast-paced, achievement-driven society, the people who get ahead are those who are diligent, hard working and energetic; not those who are idle, sluggish, slothful or resistant to exertion.

Yet, in all of the daily frenzy of a modern life, people are not only mentally unfocused and physically exhausted, but also have forgotten why they are doing so much running around in the first place. People spend a good deal of time doing, and very little time relaxing, stopping or simply being. I believe that in order to be truly happy and successful, you must learn to unplug and create a more rhythmic life that balances work with resting the body, mind and spirit.

Sounds simple, yet, how do you really reduce your speed? First, be aware of the signs indicating a respite is needed. Recurring or obsessive thoughts, being stuck on a problem that's not getting resolved, experiencing creative blocks, scheduling or planning every moment, lacking in joy, getting physically sick or run down, or feeling depressed and lethargic are all indicators that you need to slow down. Second, be aware of the reasons keeping you from taking time off. Get rid of the silly excuses and make a choice to take care of yourself first. And finally, replace old patterns with new ways of unplugging. Since everyone needs something different, listed below are some specific suggestions.

Ways to Unplug and Be Lazy:

Work Take a break from your desk and/or telephone and be "unreachable" for 15 minutes. Walk outside, read something for fun, or go to a coffee shop. If you don't already do this, go out for lunch. Leave your office messy (on occasion). And, use all of your vacation time, even if you stay home and do nothing.

Money Give yourself a break from constantly watching the stock market or your bank account balances. Create a reserve, and set aside "fun" money. If you do the bill paying, ask your spouse to do it or hire an assistant.

Body Wellness Make your movements slow and deliberate; saunter instead of rushing. Choose slower activities such as yoga or walking. Engage in nurturing activities such as baths or massages. Eat in silence and savor every bite. Turn off the alarm clock, especially on the weekends.

Friends & Family Take time off from being the planner, organizer or hostess by allowing others to take the lead. Set boundaries, when needed. Schedule a "Pajama Day" with the family. Imitate your children's playful patterns.

Romantic Partners Let go of old resentments and bad habits. Take a break from "nit-picking" and overlook your mate's shortcomings, even if it's just for a day. Make a date by staying in and inviting your partner to be lazy with you.

Spiritual Growth Cultivate an inner laziness to create peace and calm. Stop fretting and worrying. Let yourself fall asleep when you pray or meditate. Enact the Sabbath as a day of rest. Trust God or your Higher Power. Be comfortable with and ask for alone time. Journal. Be in the moment. Daydream.

Playtime Plan nothing and see what you feel like doing; follow your energy. Choose low-maintenance playmates. Select activities that require you to slow down: float in a pool, take a blanket to the park, lie in a hammock, spend time in nature, get lost in a romantic novel, watch movies in bed, play board games, read poetry or listen to classical music.

Home Take a day off from chores and let your house get messy for a few days. Hire a housekeeper. Simplify, de-clutter and create comfortable places to relax in your home. Create technology-free zones.

In his book *Sabbath*, Wayne Muller writes, "Sabbath is a way of being in time where we remember who we are, remember what we know and taste the gifts of spirit and eternity." By being lazy, you can get re-energized for the necessary work and create space to honor a period of rest that will restore you to your essential greatness.

An Exercise that Gives You Permission to Halt:

1. From the above list, choose three areas to renew yourself. Determine your *easiest* ways to rest and rejuvenate.

2. Schedule relaxed, carefree, lazy and unstructured time off. When will you take a break... today? This week? This month?

3. Decide if you will slow down with or without another person. Who will be lazy with you?

4. Make a written commitment to yourself to be lazy.

(See Excavive™ "Permission Slip" in the Appendix.)

Free Yourself

July 2009

> "We must be free not because we claim freedom, but because we practice it."
> William Faulkner

What makes a person free? As we approach our country's independence celebration, I often think about what freedom actually means. America was founded based on the desire for individual freedom, and we live in a country that provides enormous liberty, limitless opportunities and advantageous privileges. Yet, as individuals, I observe many people who do not feel free within the lives they have created. Sometimes they feel locked into their circumstances, restricted by their choices, and are scared to even question their lives, much less begin making changes.

But what if you could feel free to start living the life you are really meant to live? Have you ever thought about what it would be like to have complete and utter freedom? Do you know what freedom means to you? I have come to realize that "freedom" carries many different meanings. For some, it is the freedom to be who you are, or the freedom to express yourself fully without holding back and worrying about the consequences. Freedom can also be defined as the ability to travel, to explore the world, to learn about yourself and to connect to others.

Another way to think about having freedom is by making choices *within* the life you have already created. For example, being able to have a job you love as opposed to the one that brings in the paycheck or being able to do something for yourself if the primary focus has always been on helping others. Or even having the ability to pursue other interests or hobbies, without always feeling like there is not enough time, money or opportunity to engage in what you want, much less enjoy it.

I believe freedom is about knowing that you have choices, no matter what the circumstances. No one can take away your thoughts, feelings, beliefs, attitudes, dreams or perspectives. You have the autonomy to believe what you do, think what you want and feel what you feel without any restrictions. It is your free will and human right.

I hear people say, "I don't have a choice." It might be true there are certain responsibilities, commitments or situations that might need to be honored, or something has been handed to you that you might not have preferred. Yet, I believe you can dream of new possibilities and start making decisions to see things in a different light or do something in a new and different way.

Ways to Find Your Freedom:

What holds you back? What are the thoughts, the stories you make up, the boxes you put yourself into that hold you back and keep you from being authentic? What do you want more of in your life?

"The Let Go's"
- Freedom to Let Go
- Freedom from Stress, Worry and Anxiety
- Freedom from "Shoulds"
- Freedom from Low Self-Esteem or Self-Deprecation
- Freedom from Negativity
- Freedom from Being Defensive
- Freedom to Make Mistakes and Start Over
- Freedom from Fear
- Freedom from Doubt
- Freedom from Shame & Guilt
- Freedom to Cut Loose
- Freedom from Past Disappointments
- Freedom from Unrealized Dreams or Goals
- Freedom from Conformity
- Freedom from Disconnecting, Disassociating and Unavailability

"The Move Towards"
- Freedom of Choice
- Freedom to be Who You Are
- Freedom to Love
- Freedom of Expression
- Freedom of Self-Confidence

- Freedom to Explore
- Financial Freedom
- Freedom to Learn and Attain Knowledge
- Freedom of Our Own Thoughts, Feelings and Emotions
- Freedom to Take Action
- Freedom of Acceptance and Peace
- Freedom of Human Rights
- Freedom to Speak Up
- Freedom of Connection
- Spiritual Freedom

It is within your power to become as free and happy as you make up your mind to be. You might not be able to make immediate changes in your life at this moment, but you can start dreaming and working towards something new. Better yet, you can free yourself by changing the viewpoint or perspective you currently hold. After all, you are as happy as you decide to be—and you can start that now.

A Coaching Exercise to Free Yourself:

1. Using the list above, define what freedom means to you.

2. What do you need to free yourself from, and in what areas of life do you need relief?

3. How many ways do you know to free yourself? In other words, what will liberate you?

4. Once you have discovered of what you need to let go, you will have the freedom to go toward something new. What would you choose in any given moment?

Feed Your Soul: A Recipe for Creating a Fulfilling Life

August 2009

"People say that what we're all seeking is a meaning for life. I don't think that's what we're really seeking. I think what we're seeking is an experience of being alive, so that our life experiences on the purely physical plane will have resonances within our innermost being and reality, so that we actually feel the rapture of being alive."
Joseph Campbell

Are you living a full, rich and meaningful life, or are you depriving yourself from the aliveness and joyfulness life has to offer you? Do you feel completely satiated and satisfied, or are you starving your soul? What is your prevalent mood—one that is positive, happy and hopeful, or are you suffering from negativity, fear and dissatisfaction?

In times of unrest, it is easy to become fearful of what is either happening to us personally or to those around us. "Doom and gloom" is everywhere, and people are genuinely starving, losing self-confidence and experiencing a withering of their spirit. It seems many people have gone from over-indulgence to deprivation and, in that process, lost perspective of who they are, where they are going and what is most important. People are living in the extremes, and when this happens, it is difficult to maintain nurturing that feeds the soul and balance that honors the body, mind and spirit.

The Life Coaching process assists people in creating a unique formula for their lives, based on visualizing what they want, identifying values, creating meaningful work and moving through limiting beliefs towards peace, harmony and vitality. When all of this is mixed together, a recipe for true fulfillment and success is created, not based on something you can attain or own, but rather something you can become... your true essence.

Recipe for Creating a Fulfilling Life:

This recipe will assist you in examining your current life, claiming who you are, defining what you want more of and beginning a life focused on what makes you come alive and feel joyful every day.

Ingredients & Utensils Needed:

Your journal or several sheets of blank paper
Your favorite writing instrument
Inspiring music or quiet solitude
A designated time for reflection, at least an hour or two
A comfortable place to sit, think and write
A relaxed body, open mind and unbounded heart
A spiritual connection or time in nature
The following Coaching exercise

Directions:

Step 1: Create the time and space for contemplation. Get the distractions handled, such as turning off the phone, stepping away from the computer or waiting until the house is empty. Set aside any negativity for the moment.

Step 2: Sit quietly for a few minutes and acknowledge how wonderful you truly are. Write down what you love about yourself and for what you are grateful.

Step 3: Next, excavate your answers to these questions:

- What fills you up and nourishes you?
- When are you most alive—who are you, what are you doing, who are you with and what's happening around you?
- List your passions.
- What are your greatest gifts and talents?
- What holds you back?
- What's really important about how you live?
- Are you performing meaningful acts and being of service to others?
- Are you living well every day and practicing self-care?
- What do you REALLY want?

Step 4: Think about an experience in your life that was gratifying and brought you immense joy.

Step 5: From the answers above, extract any common themes or principles that exist and list those. Your values should be a reflection of who you are. What actions do you currently take that are life affirming and validate you are going in the right direction?

Step 6: Consider what is missing in your life that keeps you from seeking robust experiences, going after your deepest desires and experiencing happiness in your work and relationships? Name the things that hold you back and discard any self-defeating behaviors.

Step 7: Daydream and be open to all possibilities. Ask yourself again what you deeply want and then record what you are thinking. Where do you want to be next year, in five, 10 or even 20 years? Record your goals, confirm your commitments and find ways to begin.

Step 8: Reflect on how you are caring for your emotional, mental, physical and spiritual health—is it aligned with who you are and what you need?

Step 9: Seek support and enlist advocates to help you get where you want to go.

Step 10: What two steps could you <u>immediately</u> take to move you towards your plans, and begin with those items?

It is possible to have a happy life NOW with wherever you are on your current journey, including handling any stress or challenges you are currently facing. Unearth your values; feed your body, mind and spirit every day; tame the gremlins; fulfill your unique life purpose; and seek compelling approaches to all of your tasks.

The key ingredient of fulfillment is to commit to your life and create your own definition of success. Taste every morsel of your existence and savor each moment of it. Make plans to authentically grow, change and transition into a life that has rich meaning, soulful purpose and ecstatic joy. Start feeding your soul with what it truly wants, needs and desires because, after all, you are what you eat.

Do-Overs: Let Go of Your Regrets

September 2009

> *"Regrets are as personal as fingerprints."*
> Margaret Culkin Benning

Ever wish you could do "it" over? Live in another home, city or country; drive a different car or make an out-of-the-ordinary purchase; study something else or pursue an alternative career? Do you wish you married your first love, or put more effort into a friendship that ended? Do you spend your time on a daily basis thinking about what you could have said or done to comfort a loved one but didn't; overreacted by yelling or saying something you did not mean; or perhaps, you were not clear about how to respond to someone or something so you botched it and now are worried and are constantly replaying it in your head?

The regrets in your life can keep you stuck. These misgivings can build up to where they weigh you down, and, over time, the more weighed down you are, the more difficult it becomes to move forward. So what qualms still plague your mind? What decisions or lack thereof still haunt you? The keys to taking the load off and starting fresh are to relinquish your past mistakes and disappointments, to let go of guilt and sadness, and to forgive yourself. Change your perspective so you can create a new way of seeing in order to make room for a new definition of happiness. And, when necessary, have a do-over.

Do-overs can take the form of changing a specific aspect of your life, or even going back to someone to make a simple apology. Lost time can never be recovered, and your words or actions can never be completely taken back once they have been delivered. You might unintentionally hurt someone's feelings, not show your appreciation or inadvertently disappoint another; yet, you can make amends and change current behaviors into more loving connections. Here are some guidelines on knowing when you need a redo.

A Do-over is Needed When...

- it allows you to learn more about who you are and what is important to you.
- your own dreams and desires become crystal clear, and you now need to take a different path.
- you need to apologize or make an amends to another person.
- forgiveness and compassion are more important than being right.
- it allows you to face a re-occurring fear so you can be more powerful.
- you change your mind or decide to go a different direction and it impacts others.
- it teaches you to be open, honest and vulnerable in order to create intimacy.
- you need to set boundaries for future healthier interactions.
- you learn new information that changes a current perspective or viewpoint.
- it allows you to practice speaking your truth and therefore builds more self-confidence.
- you are ready for a new beginning or fresh start.

I believe do-overs give you the chance to start fresh and discover what you truly want. They provide learning opportunities to create more inner peace and harmony in your relationships and design the experiences in life you will truly treasure. A do-over can enhance your confidence, and perhaps even open the door to receive something you may not have been truly ready for in the past. A life full of conscious, proactive choices can turn our biggest regrets into our greatest adventures.

Coaching Steps to Turn Your Biggest Regrets into Visualized Actions:

Do you let yesterday's regrets use up too much of today's opportunities? What will you do to change that for yourself?

1. Make a list of your deepest, biggest regrets.

2. Using the list above, probe deeper by asking yourself how you feel today. Are there items on the list that you still desire and want to pursue; or perhaps, is it time to let go of past disappointments or unfulfilled wants?

3. Continue the process by asking the following questions:
- What is the learning opportunity?
- Is there another way to create the desired experience NOW?
- Do you need to apologize or make an amends in order to put something to rest?
- Do you need to focus on the positives instead of the "what ifs?"

4. Create a new vision of what you NOW want. Ask yourself, will these items create a sustainable "essence" of what you want long-term, i.e., greater intimacy with a partner, a more fulfilling career, creative inspiration for a passionate pursuit, or greater compassion for others?

5. Now, what action items are you willing to take to get what you want for yourself that are based on your new dreams?

6. Finally, choose the one item that speaks to your soul and do that one first.

What Goes Around Comes Around: Take Responsibility

October 2009

"If you don't tell the truth about yourself you cannot tell it about other people."
Virginia Woolf

"How people treat you is their karma; how you react is yours."
Wayne Dyer

In thinking about karma, I have been considering what it really means. I hear people use the word often, and it appears to me, there are many interpretations floating around. For instance, karma seems to have become pop culture's word for rationalizing the good or bad things that happen to us. I sometimes hear phrases like "It must be karma," meaning destiny or positive outcomes; "That's my karmic debt," implying pre-destination; or "She must have bad karma," signifying bad luck.

According to Dictionary.com, karma is one's fate or destiny. The Western interpretation based on the Christian concept of karma is about "reaping what you sow." A more Eastern approach views the effect of karmic deeds as shaping the past, present and future, as well as the karma representing our "life lesson" or "karmic debt" from something bad that we did in a past life, and we are working off the transgression in this life in order to transform or become enlightened.

Based on the many traditions and modern-day perspectives, it is no surprise that the word "karma" is overused, abused or the catch-all phrase when there is not a reasonable explanation for why something happens. Are people trying to chalk things up to "karma" as a way of not dealing with issues or to make meaning out of not having enough valid information to discern what is really happening? Is karma being used as an explanation when people are stuck in life-long patterns such as addictions, relationship issues, money problems and other serious life challenges?

In my opinion, it does not matter what definition you choose because the point is that karma asks you to change in order to heal. It asks you to take responsibility NOW for your past and present actions, and change your behaviors going forward. To me, karma in its simplest form is about cause and effect, and understanding how your choices impact not only your life path, but also other people around you.

You are in charge of your current thoughts, beliefs, decisions and ultimate actions; there is a natural consequence for your choices. You have the power to determine what kind of influence you want to have—good or bad—on yourself, others and the world at large. What goes around comes around, and you are fully responsible for changing your patterns, determining the quality of your relationships, deciding what your life can look like and how your destiny will unfold. Here are some ways to conduct more conscious deeds.

Take Responsibility for Your Actions by...

- telling the truth
- learning from your mistakes and not repeating them again
- causing no harm to others
- saying what you REALLY think, want and need by expressing your feelings
- self-checking your real intentions and motivations
- not making excuses or blaming others when you really have a part
- loving without attaching or judging
- being compassionate
- not projecting your pain on others
- letting go of false expectations
- releasing the outcomes as much as possible
- asking for help when you need it
- practicing forgiveness
- treating others as you want to be treated
- setting realistic boundaries
- wanting more for others than for yourself (it comes back to you!)
- admitting your failures and starting over, if needed

In his book *The Four Agreements*, Don Miguel Ruiz offers four simple, yet powerful, ways of creating personal freedom, responsibility, and ultimately, true happiness. Be Impeccable with your Word, Don't Take Anything Personally, Don't Make Assumptions and Always Do Your Best... these Four Agreements, when applied, can assist in creating positively powerful thoughts and behaviors. It is up to you to take full karmic responsibility for what happens next. After all, what goes around does indeed come back around sooner or later.

Purposeful Coaching Questions to Help Change Your Behaviors:

Create awareness and begin the process of change by answering the following questions. If you cannot move forward on your own, always seek outside help through therapy, coaching or a 12-step program.

1. In what life patterns are you currently stuck? What is creating your reality today?

2. What behaviors do you tend to keep repeating, never fully making the necessary changes or tough decisions to affect lasting change?

3. Make a list of everything about which you are resentful. Now consider your "part" in each item you identified. In what ways are you angry with yourself? Perhaps you are going against your values, or not using your voice.

4. What is a powerful interpretation of your current situation or dilemma? And, what is the positive result you want to create?

5. It is time to let go of the past, forgive yourself and others, and make intentional changes to your behaviors. Decide how you can be extraordinary now, and start there.

Make Space

November 2009

"Deep within your soul there is a knowing place...a sanctuary where gifts are nurtured. Enter that space. Spend time there tending your gifts. There in the chapel of your heart, you will become a gift to be given."
Anonymous

In thinking about space, my first thought was to write about cleaning out the clutter in your physical spaces; getting rid of the things and stuff that no longer work in order to make room for something else. Often when people want more, new, different or upgraded things, they believe they need to make space first, only to realize months or years later, they have simply accumulated more unwanted or useless material goods that are collecting dust and encumbering a room. The cycle continues, and another clean out is needed.

Space is most often perceived in the physical realm, but I believe there are other areas of life where clutter is held. In order to become freer and lighter overall in life, all spaces need to be considered on an on-going basis. These include not only the physical, but also the mental, emotional, relational, financial and spiritual parts. Space, which encompasses all of these areas, is the bigger vision and purpose of your life; the particles are the details, the fears, bad habits, patterns or the things in which people tend to get caught.

So, in order to create a rich, genuine vision that will move you toward all you want, you must be willing to clean up life's particles and detailed clutter, as well as keep space open and unencumbered. It is only then, with a trustful openness and new plan, you can create the space to add something back. Learning to include the pauses of life, spacing out for a while, letting go of any attachments, finding happiness with less, and being okay with the unknown are all important to the clean up process.

It is in this stillness and spaciousness that new ideas can arrive easily and serendipitously, and greater possibilities can be born.

Life Areas to Free Up More Space

Consider what you can do to make room for not only what you deeply desire but also for something better than you could possibly imagine at this point in time.

Physical Space Does your physical environment inspire you or drain you? Simplify, de-clutter and create a personal sanctuary in your home and office. What "things" are you holding on to that you really no longer need, or someone else could use more than you? Donate to charities, non-profits or consignment shops. A consistent business practice I have is when a client moves on to live their authentic journey, I take their file out of my active storage cabinet so that way I make room for new people to engage my services. New people come along at just the right moment in time, so my file cabinet is not over, or under, stuffed.

Mental Space What do you think about on a consistent basis? Are you productive, positive and proactive in your thinking, or do you have a tape running in your head over and over again, only to find that you are not really resolving anything, but merely creating a bigger problem instead of truthful solutions? Don't let your unruly thoughts run the show. Get rid of the junk in your mind so that you can be intellectually engaged and openly stimulated. Do a Brain Dump exercise on a regular basis. (See the "Brain Dump" Exercise in the appendix.)

Emotional Space How are you feeling today? Become emotionally intelligent and understand how your emotions drive your thoughts and actions. Learn to name and accept all of your emotions, as they simply are indicators that a change might be needed. Observe them, let them flow through and then use them to create new or different actions. "This Too Shall Pass" can be a great reminder.

Relational Space Do you have real connections with people who honor you and vice versa? Perhaps you need to recalibrate, rebalance or give someone space so each of you can remain true to yourself. Let go of past relationship issues, defense mechanisms, masks and bad patterns so you can allow more intimacy in a current partnership, or make space for a new relationship to blossom. What firm commitment and courageous communication can you make to the people who matter most to you, whether they are a romantic partner, family member or friend, and would like to invest in a stronger association? Take time to have communion with those you love and care for, including yourself.

Financial Space Do you use your money mindfully? Are you maximizing your hard-earned dollars and being thoughtful with your resources? Do you have debt that creates shame and guilt, or have you become financially dependent on someone else and don't know how to break free? Money is energy, so take the steps to clean up anything that is not positively working for you in this area, such as cutting frivolous spending, saving more, creating a financial plan or seeking sound advice.

Spiritual Space Do you feel connected to God or your Higher Power? Are you making the space to get spiritually grounded, be in the moment, tap into your intuition, and hear the small voice inside that sheds light in every life situation? Take time to get quiet, pray, meditate, worship, cultivate an inner peace, and renew spirit. Real "inspiration" originates from this spiritual connection.

By making space in your life to deal with the painful disappointments, the heartaches, the clutter or unnecessary stuff, you can re-energize for the necessary work, and embrace the authentically creative version of yourself. The Reverend Michael Beckwith said, "We are pushed by our pain until we are pulled by our vision." Deal with any pain or disappointments so you can move towards dreams that are full of surprises and amazing beyond your expectations. Contemplate, imagine, get spaced out, have your head in the clouds, dream with your eyes wide open and make space for your new vision.

A Coaching Exercise for Making Space for a New Vision:

Using the above areas, commit to yourself to make space by choosing an area or two to focus on, and then ask yourself the following questions:

1. If I am at my best, what would I do right now?

2. Where am I suffering? What am I resisting?

3. Where am I selling myself short?

4. What is it to surrender and be fully present?

5. What is it to engage the heart and soul?

6. What would it be like to transcend_____, in order to create_____?

Now consider creating a visual reminder that reflects what you want your life to really look like. Daydream, meditate, journal, discuss your ideas with a friend, flip through magazines, surf the internet and then construct your Vision Board utilizing words and pictures to reflect your new vision. Remember that by opening up the needed space, you will begin to see what is truly possible.

Excavate Your Creative Self

December 2009

> "The aim of art is to represent not the outward appearance of things,
> but their inward significance."
> Aristotle

When I attended my first Life Coaching training in 2003, one of the first things I learned is that everyone is "creative, resourceful and whole; and they have their answers inside themselves." [2] I understood people were fully capable of finding solutions but what I did not recognize at the time is how powerful and provocative tapping into one's creative source can be.

For many people, their creativity takes a novice approach of doing artistic things when there is extra time, money and resources. Participating in an occasional art class, taking up a new hobby, redoing your home, taking photographs or dabbling in some out-of-the-ordinary projects at work are secondary to life's bigger demands of work, family and other obligations. So, creative pursuits are not prioritized and do not hold much importance.

Others hold a dream, or are engaging in, the professional option of being an artist, designer, innovator, director, writer or trendsetter. Many of these creative types have a natural inclination or talent, are educated or trained in one or many specialties, are paid for their products and services and continually engage in their artistry.

---

2   Whitworth, Laura; Kimsey-House, Henry; Sandahl; Co-Active Coaching, Mountain View, Davies-Black Publishing

A final perspective on creativity lies somewhere in the middle where creativeness is part of everyday life and work, whether it is inventing new approaches to the current way of doing things or prioritizing at least one artistic endeavor because of the enjoyment it brings. No matter where people fall on the originality scale, I believe everyone can reap enormous benefit from finding their own creative identity which is fundamental to being able to tap into passion, joy, and deep satisfaction. It only takes courageous confidence to move forward. So, where do you start? What does it take to awaken the dormant, creative soul?

Begin by getting self-empowered to use your imagination and dream about what you want to do next. Discover what you like and dislike; establish an expansive way of thinking outside of the box; utilize consistent habits that support your vision; nurture your inner inventor; commit to staying on the chosen path even when it gets hard; have creative collaborators for renewal and accountability; build a tool kit of supplies and resources so you are always prepared to capture your inspirations; and take forward-moving action each day. By engaging in these steps, you will set in motion a more colorful and vivid life.

15 Questions to Excavate Your Creativity:

As you consider your own creative talents, it is important to give thought about how you tap into your own resourcefulness and claim what you want to create. The following questions are designed to stimulate your thinking about what ignites your passion and how your interactions in the world affect what you create.

1. What do you create and why?

2. From where do you get your inspiration and ideas?

3. How does your life reflect your creativity...in your home? Clothes? Hobbies? Relationships? Business?

4. What **unique** skills do you have that directly support your creativity? Name at least three.

5. What experiences make you feel most alive? List your passions.

6. How does color affect you? What colors do you like/dislike?

7. Think about when you are being your most creative…now describe your surroundings.

8. Do you have any "rituals" that prepare you for your project?

9. When is the best time of day for you to create?

10. Who supports your creativity? Do you have creative collaborators?

11. What distractions exist in your life that keeps you from being your most inspired self? List the things you do instead of creating.

12. How do you motivate yourself to get started on (or finish) a project?

13. Is there a common theme or element in your writing, designs, products or art?

14. What does your creativity say about you and how is it revealed in what you create?

15. What is the message you want to give your family, friends, community and the world through your creations?

Using your answers to the above questions, consider what creative projects you want to undertake. Identify two or three, choose the most provocative one, and initiate your new creative journey.

When you begin to recognize the things in your life that inspire you, you will begin to move more rapidly toward those things, and create a synergy that allows your creativity to remain ever-present, alluringly alive and permissively playful. There is an artist inside of you and you only need to excavate the truest form of your own creativity. German physicist Albert Einstein said, "Imagination is more important than knowledge." I invite you to go on an inventive quest to learn about your creative self, and then pursue the ingenious things that make you happy.

Dream in Color

January 2010

"You see things as they are and you say, 'Why?'
But I dream things that never were, and I say, 'Why not?'"
George Bernard Shaw

"Our truest life is when we are in dreams awake."
Henry David Thoreau

I love the color (or non-color) white... my favorite wardrobe pieces are my white jeans and T-shirts, as they serve as a great foundation for any outfit. My preferred jewels are my pearls because I love their feminine softness and how they remind me of the beach and their sea-origins. I crave white spaces on a page when I read a book or design my marketing materials because it emphasizes what is really important. I adore how my neighborhood looks just after the first snow when everything is fresh and beautiful. And, I am partial to white walls in my home because they are soothing and allow me to highlight my brightly-colored art (except for the time I painted my office bright pink after my divorce to signify my feminine independence and the bold change in my life that was taking place... it is now white again).

For some people, too much white can be either blinding or boring. Yet for me, using white by itself can symbolize a divine-like quality of purity, peace, comfort and stillness... a space I often crave with the busyness of life. But I also love color and I use these white foundations to serve as a neutral backdrop to enhance a mood, ignite creativity, highlight something meaningful or provide a place to launch a fresh start.

As the initiation of a new year is celebrated, I love the idea of being given a clean slate. What if you could truly have a crisp new beginning, with the purity and innocence of no fear and then boldly add as many colors to your white, blank canvas? How would your artwork unfold as you set annual goals, embrace resolutions, instill positive intentions and move bravely forward? What dreams and desires do you have for yourself this year? How would you design your new work of art, the masterpiece of your life?

Artist Vincent Van Gogh said, "I dream my painting and then I paint my dream." A new vision starts with your thoughts, hopes and aspirations, and adding your favorite colors can greatly enhance the picture you are creating in your life. Like music, color can be nourishing, uplifting and stimulating, and when positively experienced, can feed your soul and enhance your well-being. Bring inspired hues into the life areas you are drawn to; wear the colors that make you feel good; surround yourself with shades that inspire you and choose colors to best reflect your personal statement. Here are some ideas.

10 Vibrant Colors to Create a More Colorful Life:

1. **Red** is the root of passion, power, purpose, stability and focus.

2. **Pink** represents the color of the heart, romantic love and is associated with healing for breast cancer patients.

3. **Orange** encourages courage, determination, procreation, self-confidence and creativity.

4. **Yellow** enhances your mental capacity, decision-making ability and personal power... why do you think legal pads are yellow?

5. **Green** is the color of universal love, self-love and compassion. It is often associated with money and abundance.

6. **Turquoise** symbolizes the things you love and want to attract into your life, your personal preferences, and is the color I chose when creating my company, Excavive™ Life Coaching, to assist others in bringing what they want into their lives.

7. **Blue** signifies peace, expression, inspiration, serenity and communication.

8. **Purple** is often seen as royalty or a connection to the Spirit, God or your Higher Power.

9. **Black** is a neutral power color—the little black dress or the power suit.

10. **White** is a combination of all colors. It epitomizes purity in its highest form and represents a higher state of consciousness and self- awareness.

Whatever colors you choose, create a life vision that is deliberate, inspiring, balanced and will move you into action. Business speaker and consultant Rosabeth Moss Kanter said, "A vision is not just a picture of what could be; it is an appeal to be our better selves, a call to become something more." Give yourself the gift of new art supplies... start with a fresh white canvas, and then use your vivid imagination to create your master life work of art using bold, vivacious colors.

Vivid Coaching Questions for a New Vision:

1. What do you want most in 2010? Think big and consider all areas of your life.

2. If your dreams and desires were put on a canvas, what would you paint?

- What colors would you use?
- What stories would you tell?
- What objects or people need to be included?

3. Get clear by recording your goals. Are they compelling enough to take bold action? Will they create stunning success and marvelous joy?

4. By achieving your vision, will your vitality be expanded? If so, get started. If not, keep imaging and envisioning until you paint the picture for which you truly long.

Embrace Your Inner Dude

February 2010

> "To give anything less than your best is to sacrifice the gift.
> Steve Prefontaine

Women, generally speaking, are kind, compassionate, patient, nurturing, generous, sweet (most of the time) and tend to provide unconditional love. Yes, we are the soft souls that provide the heart-warming gentleness to our families, friends and partners. Yet, we can be doormats, suffer in silence, become martyrs to our circumstances, and tend to put our lives on hold—all for the sake of others. Don't get me wrong, I think women are amazing at juggling it all, and mostly being successful at it. Yet, we sometimes lack the drive, self-confidence and gumption men seem to pull off so easily.

One of the recurring themes I coach on is assisting women in rebuilding their confidence, self-worth, value and self-esteem. It seems to be a bigger issue with women than men. For example, last year I worked with a client on creating strategies for her to ask for a raise. She made the comment that other men in her office had asked for what they wanted easily, directly, expectantly, unemotionally, without hesitation and had a sense of detachment that translated into "of course I am worth it." They got what they wanted. So, I suggested that she take the same approach, and not only was it effective, but it was also easy.

This leads me to ask the questions, what can you learn from your male counterparts? How can you aggressively go for what you really want and vanish the victimization? Isn't it time to stop over-analyzing and get going? I think some of the answers can be found in lessons you can learn from guys, thereby, "embracing your inner dude."

<u>Here are some of the "Macho" Traits to Grip and Take On:</u>

<u>Persuasive Power</u> Men are natural born leaders, and do not question their individuality. They have the ability to use not only their external resources, but also access and activate their internal gifts and talents. Take the initiative, get empowered and use that power to create greatness.

<u>Physical Strength</u> Men stay committed to being active through working out and athletic endeavors to keep up their physical well-being, youthful energy and stress relief.

<u>Rational Reasoning</u> Men are less emotional when processing things, and would never cry in the face of adversity. They are able to be objective, see the bottom-line and tend to be much more logical and practical.

<u>Bold Bravery</u> Men have the courage gene. Even if they are scared, it is not as obvious, especially when it comes to going for what they want both personally and professionally.

<u>Basic Simplicity</u> Men know who they are and what they do. Plain and simple. It's not complicated for them.

<u>Decisive Assertiveness</u> Men put their stake in the ground and continue moving towards that truth. Men seem to make a decision and move on, where as women tend to dwell on decisions and question themselves after the fact. Stand up for what you think is right, and say it out loud with confidence, effectiveness and intensity... and don't look back.

<u>The Lighter Side</u> Lighten up... dudes don't worry as much. Keep it simple and consider giving up the agony of decision-making, guilt, shame and attachments.

<u>Action-Based Opportunities</u> Men generally want things to move along and go forward. They don't ask for permission; they take action, adjust, and keep going so as to not miss out. If needed, they will ask for forgiveness later.

<u>Sense of Adventure</u> Men follow their urges and are playful, spontaneous, independent, sexual and free-spirited. They say when, not if.

The Visionary Men tend to hold a big picture vision, are success-oriented, see where they are going and what it will look like when they get there. Their vigilance and focus is unshakable and allows them to stay on task.

It is not my intent in this column to over-generalize or segregate the sexes, but rather to provoke thought and learning from each other. I am not suggesting that you stop being who you are or give up the goodness that already exists, as everyone needs both energies. There is no right or wrong with the sexes, just differences to embrace. The key is to integrate the best qualities of both men and women. And, the truth is, men have a strength and power that women often struggle with owning, and with a little work, they can harness and transform their own power into productivity and prominence.

A Coaching Exercise to Excavate Your Maleness:

1. Think about two or three dudes whom you admire or who motivate you? What qualities do they possess of which you would like more?

2. When and to whom do you give your power away? Is there an opportunity to use some "male" traits to change this dynamic? Choose one bold characteristic, and practice it as much as possible.

3. Now, balance your life by fully integrating your masculine and feminine traits in as many areas as possible. Assess where you are now, decide what you need and what your new "normal" needs to be. Ask for what you want from yourself and others, using ALL the traits needed to be your best you. Some examples... do you need to be:

•   More vocal at home?
•   More caring at the office?
•   More self-assured in your relationships?
•   Bolder in your creativity?

4. Choose three brave strategies that will strengthen your self-esteem and start implementing those today.

5. Finally, and most importantly, don't forget to thank the men in your life OFTEN... they need to feel appreciated for all that they do to support you and your greatness.

Clean it Up: Keep Your Side of the Street Clean

March 2010

"Turn your wounds into wisdom."
Oprah Winfrey

In thinking about this month's dirt issue, I was brought back to one of my favorite childhood memories of making mud pies at my grandparent's house. What a lovely remembrance of my sister and I getting our hands dirty and making beautiful creations with the ingredients of nature. We spent hours playing outside knowing it was okay to get soiled and be messy. No matter how filthy our hands, faces, clothes and work areas would get, we understood that we had to clean it all up before dinner and our parents' pick-up time. Although my grandmother, Mema, would work her magic in freshening us up (she always had a hot bath waiting for us), we still had to be responsible for our carefree afternoon of messiness by cleaning up as much as we could on our own.

What I love about this story is the importance of having fun in life, and realizing there can be much playfulness, fun and creativity in getting down in the dirt of all life has to offer. Those timeless afternoons provided a great sense of aliveness, playfulness and risk-taking that adults sometimes forget. It is also a great reminder that although being grubby and carefree instills creative playtime and rich experiences, it is still necessary to clean up the disarray before you can go on to what is next. For instance, it is important not to take hurt or disappoint into the next relationship, or create false expectations in the next job just because you had a bad boss in this one. And if you make a mistake or offend another person, learn to ask for forgiveness.

In my coaching practice, I witness people who have a difficult time clearing up their life situations and have become either disenchanted or dis-empowered. Their unhappiness has been created from misunderstandings; a lack of clear communication; made-up assumptions and stories; fear of hurt, disappointment or disapproval; victimization; self-imposed shame, guilt or anger; and, in the process, they have sacrificed their own self-worth by trying to keep peace. And, without having the right tools or support to fix it, they avoid confronting the disorder, and situations can become irreparable.

Life is messy, and what often starts off as a good intention or connected relationship can sometimes turn bad. I am glad there is the freedom to risk participating in new endeavors; to exercise free will; to try something new and fail; and to immerse into chaos and confusion with people, places and situations. Enormous personal growth and passionate ventures have resulted. Yet, I also believe that there needs to be personal integrity, a relinquishing of the ego and a willingness to be accountable for one's role in any given situation. You cannot let things get messy without being willing to clean up your part, big or small.

I believe most people are good at heart, and they are doing the best they can under the stresses and challenges of the world today. People are not perfect, mistakes are made. Yet, many people can do a better job of "keeping their side of the street clean" by learning to take responsibility for their decisions, feelings, actions, words and the impact they have with other each other. Here are some tips on tidying up.

Tips for Keeping Your Side of the Street Clean:

- Admit when you are wrong and learn to apologize gracefully.
- Be honest with yourself and others.
- Have integrity by doing what you say you are going to do.
- Take responsibility for your own emotions.
- Consider all perspectives.
- Treat others as you want to be treated.
- Tell the truth and tell it quickly.
- Be kind.
- Set boundaries and learn to say no.
- Don't try to control, fix or change others.
- Choose happiness over being right.
- Speak up: ask for what you want and don't be a doormat.
- Don't take shortcuts or be passive-aggressive.
- Cause no harm to yourself or others, don't gossip.

- Don't keep repeating the same mistakes.
- Forgive and ask for forgiveness often.

Learn to be comfortable with making messes. Choose happiness and joy; forgiveness and compassion; openness and discernment. Say yes to you and no to the bad behavior of others. Try new things and risk failing. And, when you unintentionally cause harm to another person or make a mess of a situation, admit your shortcomings, ask for forgiveness and learn to clean up after yourself along the way.

Coaching Questions to Clean it Up:

1. Is there a current mess in your life you have been unwilling to look at or take action to clear? If so, what bold step can you take to move through the fear?

2. Who is making you mad, and what are you willing to do to make those relationships different? What are you tolerating? Where do you need to look at your behavior, or perhaps let go? Do you need to admit you are wrong or say you are sorry?

3. From the list above, choose one new helpful tool each week and practice integrating it into your life.

Know Who's Got Your Back

April 2010

"Problems can become opportunities when the right people come
together."
Robert Redford

Do you sometimes feel like you are all alone out in the world trying to
make a difference? Do you think you have to do it ALL, and that you
are the only one who truly cares about getting things done or making an
important impact—whether it's a community project, excellence at work,
building a business or even maintaining an orderly home? Do you find
that in the process of doing and giving, you become depleted, worn out
and ultimately ineffective?

There is a misperception that successful people do it all. They seem to
be independent super heroes who do everything with grace and ease, and
still have a smile on their faces. The media, mentors, teachers and other
well-intended people tell us in order to flourish, you have to work harder
and keep going at all costs.

The truth is... the happiest and most successful people know they can't
do it all and have built a life filled with an abundance of help and support
from many different people. They know how to sustain their success
because they balance their own roles with enlisting and receiving the aid of
others. They understand who's got their back, create reciprocal relationships
in which both people benefit and continually seek out supporters who align
with their mission, passion and purpose.

No matter what your role is, being successful in your life requires
leadership, confidence and discernment in order to claim what you are best
at doing, knowing when to delegate and recognizing on whom you can
count. Successful people are highly motivated, yet they realize they do not
need to be the best at everything. They trust others, let go of control, stay
open to change, and know "done is sometimes better than perfect." Most

importantly, they know how to build a stockpile of support for whatever they are trying to accomplish and boldly demand it when needed.

My best example of this was my own decision to hire my assistant, Meredith, in the spring of 2006. I had started my Life Coaching business at the end of 2003, working only part-time so I could continue to prioritize my children's needs while they were young. Yet, I began to understand that if I wanted to expand my services, I would need help. I was scared to make the commitment, not knowing if I could really afford it. Yet, I knew I had to trust that hiring an assistant, along with having a coach, a mentor, creative collaborators and emotional supporters, was the next best step, and it was. Meredith does what she is best at by handling details, while it frees me up to do what I love and am best at doing, and that is inspiring sustainable change in others. Here is a coaching exercise to assist you in building a strong foundation and your ultimate pillars of support.

A Coaching Exercise to Create Your Army of Advocates:

Do you know who's got your back? Do you know who is truly there for you, and for what situations? Let the following exercise allow you to identify and create your best support system.

1. Make a list of your biggest fans and supporters.

2. Consider the various parts of your life, and think about who supports you in each of the following areas:

    *   Personal
    *   Professional
    *   Emotional
    *   Spiritual
    *   Relationships
    *   Social/Cultural
    *   Financial
    *   Environmental
    *   Physical/Medical
    *   Community

3. Now consider anything with which you are struggling. Write down three things that bother you the most or you would like to change. What needs your attention the most?

4. Write down four people who can support you for each challenge. Where are you on the list?

5. Think about one thing each of these people can do to support you.

6. Consider any other ways you can get your needs met (hiring someone or asking a friend vs. doing it yourself.)

7. Now, decide and ask for what you need. People do not know what you truly want unless you make a genuine request. Remember, not asking is an automatic no.

8. Don't forget that relationships are reciprocal, so say thank you, pay on time and honor the people that assist you in being authentically fabulous.

Having people who support you not only allows you to balance and expand yourself and your services, but can also establish a more creative and synergistic collaboration that might not exist otherwise. Your army of advocates can ground you, inspire you, empathize with you, love you and pick you up when needed. The power of these interdependent connections will assist in your achievements and form life-long bonds that will make the journey much more pleasurable and fulfilling along the way.

Make Your Words Stick

May 2010

> "Use every letter you write, every conversation you have, every meeting you attend, to express your fundamental beliefs and dreams. Affirm to others the vision of the world you want. You are a free, immensely powerful source of life and goodness. Affirm it. Spread it. Radiate it. Think day and night about it and you will see a miracle happen: the greatness of your own life."
>
> Robert Muller

In thinking about the bond issue, I have to admit that my first thought was Bond, James Bond. I wondered... as a predominantly women's publication, why would my editor want to do an issue on James Bond? On one hand, his sexy character represents strength, excitement, adventure, cleverness, and playfulness, yet it seemed that many of our readers might not make the connection. I quickly realized she was talking about our lasting, relational bonds, not the Bond-like character who really didn't know much at all about how to have a relationship, much less make it last.

By definition, a bond is something that binds, fastens, confines or holds together, and as human beings, there is an innate desire to seek commonalities that bring us together. We do this on many levels, from when we first meet someone and play the "who do we know in common game" to the soft whispers of slowly revealing ourselves to another person we desire getting closer to. Do you have the glue that builds long-lasting relationships? Do you bond deeply to others? Are you building intimacy by sharing your hopes, dreams, vulnerabilities and fears?

To create a solid connection with someone else, it is important to have shared experiences and a strong bonding agent through effective communication skills. Whether you have a parent/child, romantic relationship, brother/sister, family, friend, boss/employee and/or any other type of partnership... it is important to understand that one of the keys to creating unbreakable bonds is through the ability to say what you want, when you want and be heard on the other side without being reactive, withholding ourselves, or fearing judgment.

The art of learning to convey information, thoughts, feelings, desires and opinions while at the same time creating the intended impact is a skill that can be developed and nurtured. Our words, spoken or written, are powerful, and can build up or tear down. Their impact cannot be taken lightly. The right words can create trust, loyalty, commitment, enthusiasm, love, healing and a deeper bond. Think about how you feel when someone genuinely says to you "thank you," "please," "I appreciate you," "great job," "I love you" or "I'm sorry." But when the wrong words are imparted, such as "you should have..." or "I am disappointed in you," it can be devastating and a bond can be weakened or broken completely. Here are some suggestions to enhance your communication skills:

Tools to Communicating Effectively:

Exude Confidence Build a strong sense of self. Be your own best advocate. Create credibility with direct eye contact, a strong handshake and verbal connections.

Create Connection Speak from the heart. Encourage reciprocal communication so both parties have a chance to speak, be heard and honored. Learn about the other person and what's important to them.

Get Curious Ask provocative, interesting questions so you can learn as much as possible without it being an interrogation. Don't make assumptions by not asking. Be direct and clear about what you really need, want or must convey.

Listen Actively Two ears and one mouth—so listen twice as much as you speak. Stay in the present moment and don't think about your next question or idea if it causes you to not pay attention to what's being said. Ask for feedback and don't take anything personally.

Get Smart Information is power. Engage in research online, find support groups, and obtain other experts. Seek wisdom when needed.

Take Responsibility Fully own your words. Practice silence, as well as speaking up. Don't write an e-mail or text when a conversation by phone or in person is better.

Ask for What You Want Strive for clear, concise communications. Ask for what you want, and remember that not asking is an automatic NO. Your self-worth does not change from rejection—no one can take your self-esteem away except you.

Practice, Practice, Practice Speak powerfully, directly, and graciously as often and in as many life areas as possible. Use "I" statements and keep trying, keep going, don't give up—EVER. Always do your best and recognize your successes.

I believe learning to use your voice effectively is one of the best ways to build better relationships. The use of authentically communicating what you know, how you feel and what you need is one of the best assets I have discovered both personally and professionally. It is essential to use discernment, speak your truth, follow through with matched actions and show compassion and kindness to others. Leadership expert Lance Secretan was quoted in *Motto* Magazine by saying, "Authenticity is complete oneness in our thinking, speaking, feeling and doing. It's head, mouth, heart and feet all communicating and living the same message." Excavate your true voice clearly, confidently, respectfully and effectively, as it will assist in forming bonds that can last forever.

Coaching Questions to Excavate Your Voice:

1. How are you using your voice to say what you want and how you feel? Count the number of times you speak authentically each and every day until it becomes a habit.

2. Notice every time you use the word "should"… is it truly what you want or a different version of what you think you are supposed to do, say, think or feel?

3. Make your words count by only speaking powerfully this week. Why not try being Bond, Jane Bond, by saying exactly what you need to but the difference is *you mean it?*

There is No Time to Waste: Get Going

June 2010

> *"We don't have an eternity to realize our dreams, only the time we are here."*
> Susan Taylor

It's June and summer is upon us... a typical time for creating new adventures by taking breaks, visiting relatives, entertaining friends, taking up new hobbies or athletic endeavors, beginning home projects, playing outdoors, attending concerts and enjoying all life has to offer while the weather is warmer and there is a vibrant energy in the air. It is often a time when people can take time off from the day-to-day, and do something different and fun-filled. Summer also offers us the chance to fulfill our dreams... the really big ones such as taking that amazing vacation, buying our ideal home, writing a novel or having a new romance.

So, what is your heart's desire, and have you started making plans? Are you dreaming big and have you begun taking steps to make your life vision a reality? If not, what are you waiting for?

As a Life Coach, I am hired to get people moving, but in that process, I encounter people who are a victim of the "some days" or find themselves saying, "I'll get to it later," "I am too busy now" or, "After *this*, I will start *that*." Many people wait for the perfect partner, a different playmate, more money, the children to grow up, or the house to be clean. They think "I am the only one who can accomplish something, others can't do it without me or there is no one else to get 'xyz' done." Many of these people put things on hold indefinitely, make up excuses for not getting started and procrastinate, causing unnecessary stress and constant disappointment.

I understand the need to balance life's demands and responsibilities. But I wonder why so many people don't get started sooner and become fierce for their dreams. Even while visions are being created, strategies are being planned, motivation is being sought after and fear is being worked through, life continues to unfold and happen. Someone gets sick or goes away, a home repair costs more than expected or another project at work comes up. Don't get me wrong, there are often legitimate reasons why the timing is not right to move forward on a project. Waiting can be a benefit when it allows one to gather more information, adjust the vision or save more money in order to avoid debt. But when days turn into weeks, months or even years, then perhaps it is time to make a courageous change, a daring move and decide to boldly move forward anyway.

Suggestions for Moving Forward Faster:

- Start with the Big Picture in mind. What's the compelling reason to choose this?
- Prioritize. Create a Life List and make sure you ask yourself, "Is this what I want?"
- Use a Brain Dump to get out of the spinning in your head. Write everything down by thinking it and inking it. (See "Brain Dumping" coaching exercise in the Appendix.)
- Do the BIG thing first and get started. Do something, do anything, just get going. You can adjust later.
- Create structure, attainable goals and celebrations along the way.
- Make expectations real.
- Be scared and try something anyway. Face your fears and keep going.
- Learn to say no often so you can say yes to things you really want. Don't forget to ask yourself, "Is this what I want?"
- Do one task at a time, being fully present in that moment.
- Ask for help and learn to delegate—enlist others or hire someone.
- Be proactive with the tasks you need to get done instead of reacting to the demands of others.
- There is no good time and no bad time to get started when it comes to pursuing your passions, so anytime will do.

Get started, get going, just do something, anything, to move toward what you truly long for and desire. As First Lady Eleanor Roosevelt said, "Move boldly in the direction of your dreams."

It is up to you to embrace your dreams and not only wish for them, but to actively pursue making your world as big and wonderful as you want. Life continues to move forward, with or without you on board, and there are ALWAYS good enough reasons not to do something and choose to wait. However, we also do not know what tomorrow will bring us, good or bad, so really, THERE IS NO TIME TO WASTE. Tomorrow, it might be too late...so, get going today.

Coaching Questions to Get You Going:

What do you hugely desire to do, see or experience? What's going to ignite you and get you moving in a bold, fierce, "got to have it" way?

1. Define what you want, now and later. Do you have an inspiring life vision that includes fun, happiness and meaning?

2. Know the difference between a wish and a goal. Are your actions inspired by a compelling goal, or are they still hopeful wishes? What steps have you taken to move towards your dream?

3. What excuses do you make to keep you from having these things? How have you withheld yourself from life? How do you limit yourself or hold back? Name your "stoppers," and refute them, prove them wrong and deny their hold on you.

4. Powerfully interpret your current situation, and decide what you are going to do to "get going". If you were at your best, what would you do next, and go do that.

Renew Yourself: The Essential Uses of Water

July 2010

"Water is the driving force of all nature."
Leonardo da Vinci

When I first learned that H2O was selected as this month's theme, I was initially thrilled, as I love everything about water. Yet, it has been difficult to decide what to focus on since the element of water is prevalent in most parts of life... from the day-to-day habits and environmental influences to the religious practices and symbolic meanings, water is omnipresent. So, I offer you the many essential qualities and uses of water, allowing you to take what you want and leave the rest.

Water makes up roughly 70 percent of the human body and covers about three-fourths of the earth's surface. Water is everywhere, is part of everyone and is needed for almost every thing we do in life—physically, recreationally, mentally, spiritually and emotionally. For example, in my daily life, I begin and end each day with the rituals that require water such as showering in the morning to assist in being fresh, using water to carry nutrients and minerals to my body, and drinking my green tea while journaling, meditating and creating. During the day, my favorite drinks are water and iced tea, always quenching my thirst during client meetings, working out or sharing a glass of wine with a friend. And in the evening, I water my flowers to keep them beautiful and I cook dinner, which always requires the essential liquid. And finally, I often indulge in a soothing aromatic bath to relax and remove the dirt and transgressions of the day.

Water also provides the recreational backdrop for sports such as swimming, sailing, kayaking, surfing and skiing. It inspires vacation destinations for the sake of experiencing the splendor of our oceans, waterfalls, rivers, lakes and other bodies of water. By tapping into the essence of water through the five senses, life can be enriched by seeing beautiful aquatic landscapes; by listening to the soothing effects of rain drops, ocean waves or water fountains; by feeling the coolness of water directly on your skin in a bathtub, swimming pool, lake or shower; by tasting the purity of water, and finally, by smelling the unpolluted air after a rain storm.

Even as I write this column, it is raining outside, and I can't help but appreciate the nourishment the plants, trees and grass are receiving, not to mention the replenishment of our water supplies. I love the fresh air following a rain or snow storm, feeling like the air is crisper and cleaner. I am grateful for the water's ability to extinguish destructive fires, proving once again that water's cool properties are restorative. I sometimes even think that the rain represents the release of God's tears that are cleansing the many souls on this earth plane. Water is considered a purifier not only to the globe but also in most religions. Water assists in the performing of the sacraments at both the beginning and end of life such as Baptism and cleansing the dead before they are buried.

And finally, I am one of three astrological water signs, a Scorpio, along with my fellow Cancers and Pisces. As a water sign, I tend to be intuitive, emotional, intense and compassionate, and I love that I can feel the depth of my emotions and access my intuition which enables me to better connect with God, myself, my clients and other loved ones. Even when tears are brought on by sadness or hurt, water can heal the heart and release stress, thereby removing the angst.

So, how do you honor water in your life? Are you unconditionally grateful for the abundance of clean water? Are you consciously aware of the many uses water provides you, and the rituals water offers you? The best quality of water is that it helps promote relaxation, restoration, nourishment and assists in de-stressing from the day-to-day busyness of our lives. Honor the essential uses of water in your daily life by being mindful rather than wasteful with one of our greatest natural resources, water.

Let the Expansive Qualities of Water Enhance Your Life:

- **Clean** off dirt and filth
- **Cleanse** your emotions
- **Release** stress
- **Transport** nutrients
- **Purify** your spirit
- **Remove** tearful sadness or fears
- **Beautify** your landscapes
- **Activate** recreation
- **Enhance** flavors
- **Dilute** strength in order to rebalance

- **Soothe** tiredness, aches and pains
- **Nourish** your body, mind and spirit
- **Create** good food, fun and memories
- **Promote** great health

A Coaching Exercise to Integrate Daily Habits for a More Fluid Life:

When you think about your daily life, what habits do you practice on a regular basis that keep you cool, centered, pure and focused? List 10 things you are willing to do every day to cleanse, replenish, nourish and take EXTREMELY good care of yourself. These can be anything from taking a hot bath, making healthy meals, drinking more water, honoring spiritual rituals, taking up a water sport, planting flowers, making a donation towards clean water, taking shorter showers or expressing your true emotions and feelings.

My close friend and colleague James has "Bubble Bath Epiphanies" about creative ideas on a regular basis. And, some of my best creative thoughts come to me when I am showering. Make sure your habits are things that you would LOVE to do, as opposed to what you think you should do. And consider using water to enhance your self-care.

1. _____
2. _____
3. _____
4. _____
5. _____
6. _____
7. _____
8. _____
9. _____
10. _____

(See "Excavating Your Best Habits" for an expanded coaching exercise in the Appendix.)

Launch Yourself: Love What You Do

August 2010

"Don't die with your music still in you."
Wayne Dyer

Becoming an empty nester is a time when a parent's child or children are flying the coop and leaving home, maybe for the first time beyond summer camps, school trips, family visits or extended vacations. These fantastic creatures are seeking their independence and moving on to higher learning, jobs, marriages or other living arrangements, and it can be both exciting and scary. I think about the many men and women who have done their duty and put in their time as parents and caregivers, and the next possibilities for not only their children, but also their own next life cycle.

Although I am personally two years away from experiencing this rite of passage with my first-born son, both friends and clients have told me the feeling is conflicted. It can be a time of ecstatic joy and reclaimed freedom, as well as sadness, grief and loss. Sending off anything or anyone, much less our children can be bittersweet. There is an excitement of seeing children come into their own and their hard work coming to fruition by hopefully witnessing them being accepted into their college of choice or attaining their first great job. Yet for many parents, fear sets in, wondering if the values, self-confidence, grounding, self-discipline, boundaries, empathy and inspiration for their youngster's path will remain intact during the next life phase. While a certain amount of letting go, mourning, grieving, cleaning out and trust needs to be present, there can be a graceful transition into enormous opportunities to continue modeling what a great life can look like, especially by relaunching yourself.

If this applies to you, or someone close to you, you can give yourself permission to redefine life as you have known it and explore not only "what's next?" but also "what could the best possible future look like?" If your main focus has been raising your children, and that job is changing or evolving, then it is essential you deal with the emotional shifts that are occurring and be proactive during this transition time to find something new that is meaningful to you. You need to create a new norm and, ideally, have something to actively look forward to each and everyday that will engage your values, desires, creativity, interests, talents and passions. To begin, look inside yourself and ask for what your heart and soul long for.

A fresh start for anyone, not just empty nesters, could include embarking on a new career path (or re-evaluating your current job) by working in an office for camaraderie and professional meaning; starting your own business that can provide independent abundance and productive usefulness; re-igniting love by reconnecting to your spouse, yourself, old friends or a new partner; volunteering your time and resources to fight for a cause that is important to you; finding a spiritual journey that awakens, revisits or brings higher meaning into your life; going to school for specialized learning; or simply traveling the world for new experiences and adventures.

The point is to look soulfully inward, discover what you love and do that every single day. Psychologist Carl Jung said, "Your vision will become clear only when you look into your heart. Who looks outside dreams, who looks inside awakens." Create your next life vision by rousing what you want to do next. Just make sure that you authentically love it and that you actually do something about it. Here are some guidelines to stir the soul.

Loving What You Do Requires…

- Connection to your own uniqueness
- Freedom of expression
- Playful passion
- Anticipation and excitement
- Quiet confidence
- Intellectual stimulation and continual learning
- Enough challenge to hold your attention
- A higher purpose and deeper meaning
- Responsible power
- Creative opportunities and outlets
- Beautiful, inspiring and comforting surroundings
- Supportive advocates and creative collaborators
- A spacious vision with an intentional game plan
- A deep desire for something better

Sufi Mystic Rumi said, "Everyone has been made for some particular work and the desire for that work has been put in his or her heart." Look into your heart and find a deep purpose that includes richness, fullness, passion and wisdom. Find something extraordinary and then launch the next best version of you.

12 Coaching Questions to Assist Your Next Life Launch:

1. What is it to have a full, rich life?
2. What is just one more possibility?
3. If you got it, what would you have?
4. How will you know you have reached it?
5. What kind of game plan do you need to create? With whom?
6. What resources are available to you?
7. What keeps, or will keep, you going?
8. What thrills you?
9. What does your heart say?
10. What did you put on pause that you want to hit the restart button?
11. What is it to be generous with yourself?
12. What could the best possible future look like?

Take the answers to the above questions and look for the emerging themes. Give yourself permission to claim it as yours and then take inspired action steps each and every day to move towards your newly created vision.

(See "Excavive™ Permission Slip" in the Appendix.)

Honoring Your Life Cycles

September 2010

> "No road is too long for him who advances slowly and does not hurry, and no attainment is beyond his reach who equips himself with patience to achieve it."
> Jean de La Bruyere

When I learned of this month's theme, the #4 issue, I pondered, "What is the significance of the number four from a Life Coach's point of view? What could I possibly convey that would be meaningful, insightful and inspiring based on the number four?" So I did what I often do... I asked someone, and the answers started to come. My daughter Tess' response was brilliant. She explained that we celebrate endings and completions every four years... the president's term lasts four years and the Olympics are held every four years. Most people earn their high school and college diplomas in four years. And, annually, we celebrate the beginning of a new year after four seasons have been experienced. So, I started to think...why four?

The number "four" seems significant because having a designated period of time, such as the four seasons or a four-year program, allows for an entire cycle to take place, thereby allowing for optimum growth and learning. There is a natural order in life so that whatever is being created can come to fruition, fully mature and then set the stage for the next phase. There must be enough time and space for something to incubate, unfold, grow, develop, change, ripen and be established. By experiencing a complete cycle, it will bring the truest form of what is being created. This must occur in order for there to be fullness, understanding, sustainability and gestation of life.

Let's examine this further. The president takes office and he must learn the ins and outs of being our country's leader. There must be a designated period of time for the person in charge to assess the current situation, make a plan, build alliances, take action, make adjustments and hopefully achieve success for the country and its citizens. Time is needed to allow positive progress to take place.

An Olympic athlete spends four years training and developing their physical, mental and emotional selves between events in order to compete at their personal best level. Time is needed to create good habits, peak performance levels and a flow and rhythm to their specific sport. Not only are they training to be at their highest individual levels but sometimes also working together to grow as a team.

A student needs four years of higher learning so the body, mind and spirit can develop and evolve. There is a progression of learning that takes place on many levels, not just the education itself. During their studies, students deepen their knowledge of the basic subjects of reading, writing, math, foreign languages, history, the humanities and sports. But more importantly, they are learning a sense of responsibility and commitment, the development of self-confidence and self-esteem, the endurance of hard work, the value of honesty and integrity, the necessity of organization, the freedom of creativity and the expansion of critical thinking and leadership skills. They are growing up.

Like the leader, the athlete and the student, individuals who engage in a purposeful self-growth process such as life coaching or therapy are more likely to maximize their personal evolvement and create life changes that stick when they allow the full process to happen. By allowing time and space to fully complete a task, reach a goal or change a behavior, fulfillment, joy and sustainability can be achieved. The coaching process is best when there is a full sequence of evaluating the starting point, setting intentions or goals, excavating a plan, implementing inspired action, evaluating the results, recalibrating the path and starting again. Each step must be acknowledged and honored.

As novelist Katherine Anne Porter wrote, "There seems to be a kind of order in the universe, in the movement of the stars and the turning of the earth and the changing of the seasons, and even in the cycle of human life. But human life itself is almost pure chaos. Everyone takes his stance, asserts his own rights and feelings, mistaking the motives of others, and his own." Be in charge of your final destiny by choosing to grow along the way and honor your process, including completions.

Tools for Achieving Completion and Finalization:

- Know your starting point

- Decide your destination or desired final outcome
- Put an action plan in place
- Get going and try something, anything
- Slow down
- Observe and evaluate
- Process along the way
- Savor the journey
- Learn from your mistakes
- Adjust your plan
- Begin again
- When complete, fully honor the achievement

How do you honor the cycles of your life? Do you give adequate leeway for the necessary stages of growth and completion to occur? Can you stick with the ups and downs, ebbs and flows… for the sake of a full and satisfying life? In today's impatient world of hurriedness and instant gratification, there is an opportunity to slow down, be fully present and savor each stage of the journey. And, when the cycle is complete, honor what has been learned, and then start again.

<u>Coaching Questions for Completion:</u>

1. How far have you come?

2. What do you want to complete?

3. What are you learning about yourself?

4. Who are you becoming?

5. How do you want to transcend?

6. What is it to live life fully?

7. Who are you impacting or influencing?

8. What is your gift to others, to your community, and to the world at large?

9. What have you built and what is your legacy?

10. How will you honor this completion?

Get Busted: The Gift of Failure

October 2010

> "Failures are finger posts on the road to achievement"
> C. S. Lewis

I have been told that people must fail, sometimes many times, before success can be attained. There are countless stories of people who have been rejected, lost their fortunes, were told they will not amount to anything or have failed relationships, only to overcome the obstacles and find enormous success in the aftermath. So, if failure is part of the formula for success, why are people so afraid of getting busted?

Society is eager to define what success means for people, and each stage of life seems to be judged by what we do or do not do; have or do not have; and accomplish or do not accomplish. Many people fail along the way, and there seems to be harshness and judgment of those individuals in that moment. No wonder people are afraid to fall short. They are so busy worrying about what people might think that they often miss seeing the gift that failure has to offer. They are running scared from the fear of failure, sometimes more than the failure itself.

So what's the solution? Fail. Fail fast, fail hard and then tap into a deeper desire to excel and begin again. Comedian Bill Cosby said, "In order to succeed, your desire for success should be greater than your fear of failure." There is a richness and wisdom to someone who has failed and come back with inner strength, disciplined determination, gentle compassion and the knowledge that they can survive adversity. American industrialist Henry Ford realized this when he stated, "Failure is simply the opportunity to begin again more wisely."

Allow disappointment to bring you back to your true essence by stripping away any inauthentic expectations, rediscovering your solid values and going forward with what really matters most to you. When my marriage failed, it became an opportunity for me to redefine who I am and then create a career based on what really mattered to me... empowering others to be their true selves. It's probably not something I would have done without failing in the life I had created and then getting honest about what was really important to me. I had to overcome the fear of not being able to support myself emotionally, spiritually and financially in order to move forward anyway.

So I ask you, have you gotten busted lately? Has the possibility of failure entered your world and you are afraid of what will happen next? Are you shy about making a mistake, one so big that you might not survive the consequences or perhaps know what to do next? Use this opportunity to discover something bigger and better about yourself. Television pioneer and philanthropist Oprah Winfrey said, "Think like a queen. A queen is not afraid to fail. Failure is another stepping stone to greatness." I urge you to face any fear, embrace failing often so that you can wildly exceed your own expectations and receive the full benefits of living a complete life with meaning, purpose, pleasure and greatness.

Tips on Embracing Failure:

- Accept that failure is part of the process.
- Don't play the blame game– don't run or hide from your mistakes but rather clean up what is necessary.
- Make the action wrong, as opposed to the person being wrong.
- Love the lesson itself.
- Apologize for what you did, not for who you are.
- Choose staying positive with others by not spreading negativity, even during the disappointment.
- Be vulnerable, tell on yourself and be human.
- Refute any shame or guilt.
- Model failing gracefully and notice your positive personal impact.
- Be flexible and open to change.
- Draw conclusions but don't make assumptions without knowing the facts first.
- Assess rather than judge.

- Be proactive around solutions as opposed to being reactive to fear or pain.
- Create something new and wonderful from the learning, rather than staying stuck in pity.
- Don't continue the insanity by doing the same thing repeatedly.
- Look to what you did right– there are always positives.
- Determine what is next– don't stay stuck in the muck.
- See all of the possibilities and make conscious choices.
- Recover and begin again.
- Trust yourself, especially in the unknown.
- Resist shutting others out, keep the heart connection alive.
- Ask for help- it is a sign of strength and courage, not weakness and fear.
- Stay connected to your heart, to others and to your bigger vision.

In her Harvard commencement speech in 2008, the Harry Potter series author JK Rowling stated, "The knowledge that you have emerged wiser and stronger from setbacks means that you are, ever after, secure in your ability to survive. You will never know yourself, or the strength of your relationships, until both have been tested by adversity." Welcome the opportunity to get busted, and use it as opportunity to continue to transform into the real you. Even Buddha said, "The only real failure in life is not to be true to the best one knows."

Coaching Questions to Go from Failure to Empowerment:

Think about a past decision when you got busted, the current reality of a recent failure or the possibility of a looming defeat. Consider the questions below.

1. What led up to the situation and what do you make of it?

2. What did you learn about how you faced the circumstances?

3. If the same thing came up again, what would you do differently?

4. What is it to transcend your sense of failure?

5. What matters most to you now?

6. What would you attempt to do if you know you could not fail?

Embrace Beauty, Inside and Out

November 2010

> "Love of beauty is taste. The creation of beauty is art."
> Ralph Waldo Emerson

It is said that beauty lies in the eye of the beholder. Are you acquainted with what is beautiful to YOU? What stirs your senses, makes your heart beat faster and makes you smile? Do you know what makes beautiful people pretty?

Beauty can be defined as the pleasing appearance, impressive qualities and excellent aspects of someone or something. Many people are taught that looking at themselves and being concerned about physical attractiveness or a beautiful home can be shallow, selfish or in vain. However, I have always believed that taking the time to look and feel your best, as well as create beauty in everything you do, is a reflection of a strong self-esteem. Attractiveness is often focused on external appearances; yet it is equally important to cultivate your internal qualities and make it an inside job as well.

As a lover of beauty, I find that beauty must be experienced and reflected in as many aspects of life as possible. By taking the time to discover your own personal style, tastes and preferences, you can then let it emulate everywhere and in everything, especially in your looks, your surroundings, your activities, your relationships and your creations. Beauty in all its many forms must be witnessed, enhanced, preserved and shared. And what you create through your definition of beauty will be a mirror of your true essence and ultimately an inspiration to others.

Ways to Beautify Your Life

Beauty can be found everywhere in the ordinary and extraordinary. It is up to you to open your eyes, mind, heart and soul to all that is present. American professor of psychology Abraham Maslow said, " Some people have a wonderful capacity to appreciate again and again, freshly and naively, the basic goods of life with awe, pleasure, wonder and even ecstasy." Become a seeker of simple beauty, an explorer of magnificent wonders and searcher for all things good. Discover some new ways to experience beauty.

Inner Beauty:
- Find gratitude, meaning and purpose in your work
- Unleash your inner goddess
- Embrace full experiences and emotions through the chaos and order, turmoil and calmness
- Develop a strong sense of self

Outer Beauty:
- Reflect what's on the inside
- Create a healthy lifestyle to be your best
- Find your personal style
- Adorn yourself in fashion that looks good, feels good and enhances your true self
- Finish your look with a smile

Domestic Beauty:
- Fill your surroundings with things you love, honor and appreciate
- Bring nature indoors
- Add colors to your palette
- Clear as much clutter as possible
- Have at least one beautiful room that is yours

Relational Beauty:
- Nurture healthy relationships and set boundaries when needed
- Be around positive people who make you feel good
- Learn about those you admire and why you are drawn to them
- Respect others and their uniqueness goodness

Organic Beauty:
- Strive to accept what is
- Go with the flow
- Make life effortless

Sensual Beauty:
- Know what makes you feel alive and pursue those passions
- Hold hands, kiss slowly and get plenty of physical touch
- Ignite your senses

Expansive Beauty:
- Seek and expand passions, interests and visual beauty beyond the mundane
- Visit art museums, listen to live music, watch the sun rise, gaze at the stars
- Marvel at something majestic
- Dream while you are awake

Coaching Questions to Create, Experience & Reflect Your Beauty:

1. How do you define beauty? What do you appreciate most about exquisiteness?

2. What is important, or not important, to YOU about your looks, your surroundings, your things or what you create?

3. If beauty lies in the beholder, look in the mirror and ask yourself what you observe. What do you like? What do you dislike? Hold your gaze until you truly see what is gorgeous about you.

4. Think about people who appear to be beautiful. What draws you most to them? What do you notice about their demeanor, their garments, their expressions, their actions, their body language, their confidence or strong sense of self?

5. Determine what lights you up from within. When do you feel most attractive? What are you doing, where and with whom?

6. How have you withheld yourself from consistently attaining or experiencing more beauty?

7. Consider what ways you would like to add or experience more magnificence in your life… with people, places, things, or even your own creativity?

8. What have you been settling for instead of ____? Why bother? Find a good enough reason to make it pretty.

9. Finally, expand your range, richness and fullness. What is it to be truly beautiful and experience splendor? Embrace beauty by adding more pleasing and impressive qualities to your life, inside and out.

Reflect on Your Past

December 2010

"The purpose of life is to live it, to taste experience to the utmost, to reach out eagerly and without fear for newer and richer experience."
Eleanor Roosevelt

I recently attended my 30-year high school reunion in Texas, and was met with a wonderful greeting of my history. After spending a weekend with those friends who have known me the longest, and perhaps the best, I was struck with how easy it was to reconnect and be together. Except for a few wrinkles, a couple of extra pounds and many life experiences, it was as if time had not really passed as we retold our most memorable stories into the wee hours of the morning. There were only about dozen of us but a strong force of nostalgia and love was present.

As I returned home, I thought about the depth of those connections and how those wrinkles we have accumulated are hard won from our many choices, good and bad. Some crevices have been earned from the pain of stressful challenges such as divorce, death, parenting and just trying to make ends meet. Those so-called war wounds have made us all stronger and wiser. Other wrinkles, the good ones, were a tribute to well-lived lives, successful careers, lasting relationships and the expressions of those experiences through our smiles and laughter. I realized these "wrinkles" not only tell our stories but can also be a road map to heal our past, replenish our present and realign our future as we continually rejuvenate ourselves through smoothing out the painful bumps and staying connected to what's brightly important to us.

As a Life Coach, I don't delve too deeply into the past with my clients except to examine someone's peak life experiences in order to excavate their values and better determine what is important to them. By looking at their greatest joys and occasional sorrows, we are able to identify and acknowledge the sum accumulation of their best attributes and who they have become up to that present moment. From there, we can ask what's missing, what needs to be healed and then start creating the future through intentional goals and actionable items.

Those wrinkles in time inform, celebrate and encourage growth. Yet, if there is painful hurt that has not been healed, then these deep wounds can limit progress and must then be examined and let go of in order to move forward. It is through this process of forgiveness, often of both self and others, that one must successfully navigate the path towards their future. By facing what holds them back and challenging their limiting beliefs about their own personal history, they can begin to see clearly what is true today and what can be possible for tomorrow. This self-reflection is the key to connecting all the pieces of one's self: one's past, present and future for the sake of peaceful wholeness.

Tips for Reflection and Reconnection to Yourself:

The prefix "re" means to go back to the original place, to go back again. There are gifts in looking to the past in order to break any undesirable patterns or life cycles. Consider how these words can assist you in your healing and reconnecting you to you.

- **Reflect** upon your life path and how you have evolved to this point.
- **Reconnect** to your archival friends who know you best and can remind you of your greatness.
- **Remember** to be grateful to those who respect, honor and love you.
- **Revisit** your dreams and wishes. What have you wanted to do yet haven't?
- **Rejuvenate** yourself with healthy choices.
- **Replenish** good memories by seeking rich new experiences.
- **Remain** authentically true to you.
- **Reassess** if your current path is still in alignment with your future desires. What's important to you now?
- **Refuse** negativity, mediocrity, fear, old stories, limiting beliefs and the status quo if it does not empower you.
- **Refute** guilt and shame.
- **Rekindle** passionate pursuits in order to connect with a part of yourself that might be lost or forgotten.

- **Remind** yourself that living according to your values is worth it. Don't betray yourself.
- **Redefine** the seemingly impossible. Choose your future path.

There are gifts in looking to the past in order to be present to creating your future. Embrace the well-deserved age-lines and fill-in the ones that need to be smoothed out. Don't let the past control you, but rather reflect on your life's legacy and choose to love all of your wrinkles, good and bad.

Coaching Questions to Reflect Upon:

1. What do you like MOST about yourself now? What about from your past?

2. Who are you becoming?

3. How have you withheld yourself from the best life has to offer?

4. What pain still exists that instead of healing you are simply smoothing over?

5. Who, or what part of life, do you still need to forgive? Be sure to include yourself.

6. From the list above, choose one new helpful tool each week and practice integrating it into your life.

Believe

January 2011

> "The future belongs to those who believe in the beauty of their dreams."
> Eleanor Roosevelt

Here we are again... it's the beginning of another year and it is time to claim your new resolutions, another moment to set soulful goals, an additional opportunity to begin again with clearer intentions, and a renewed possibility to really achieve all that you want in your life... you know, the really, really big stuff. A new career, a fit body, a big love, financial freedom, meaningful relationships, creative pursuits. I love the process of continually re-launching a life vision by checking in on what has been accomplished, asking the questions about where you are now, and then envisioning the future based on the continual growth and learning that happens as each year passes. I am inspired by imaginative actions that lead to marvelous joy, expansive vitality and stunning success.

Yet, as I write this, I wonder, why is it that some people can stay on a clear path of manifestation and stay true to the efforts to attain their dreams with balance and ease, and others can't? What does it ultimately take to remain focused and keep going toward their aspirations when it sometimes seems unattainable, frustrating, too hard or flat out hopeless? What's the secret to the success that many people seem to have mastered, yet has completely evaded others? Is it luck and the stars finally aligning? Is it powering on with hard work and perseverance?

Those qualities can be part of the formula: claiming the vision, doing the work to back up the goal and sometimes allowing fate to play a part. But more importantly, I think the secret ingredient missing for many people is the importance of BELIEVING that you really can have what you want.

Magic happens when you can source what you want from your own heart and soul, completely believing it exists, and accepting nothing less for yourself than the best possible outcome. Believe that you and your soul mate will find each other. Trust that the career you love will bring you abundance. Accept that your friends are tried and true. Envision a healthy, fit and fabulous body. Believe you can publish a best-selling book. Confidently launch your dreams; go forward with self-assured certainty; rid yourself of fear, doubt and ego; be open to making adjustments along the way; learn to receive the good and the bad; gather support from your caring collaborators; and use failure as an opportunity to transform, learn, grow, and launch again. Prepare yourself to receive what you ask for, have faith it is on its way, continually re-launch as you gather new information and keep going each and every day, every step of the way.

Soulful Life Areas to Believe In:

As a Life Coach, I am hired to assist my clients in achieving their goals in an authentic and sustainable way that honors them as well as the people around them. I instill clarity, confidence and passion, and hold my clients accountable to their wishes. Part of the process includes examining their belief system to see if their thoughts are empowering and moving them forward, or limiting and holding them back. Examine each of the following life areas, and determine if your beliefs are best serving you.

Career & Education Do you love what you do? Are you receiving value, both monetary and recognition, for your efforts? Discover what makes you satisfied in your work and make sure the rewards match the job. If not, explore new possibilities.

Money Do you believe in abundance and that money is plentiful, or is tight and scarce? Does money come easily or does money evade you, causing you to doubt your own worth?

Health & Wellness Does your body support your life? Do you listen to your body and act accordingly? Do you create the time to instill best practices for your longevity?

Friends & Family Savor your connections by giving as much as you receive. Let the people in your life sustain you and your dreams. Do your relationships build you up or tear you down? What boundaries or different choices do you need to make?

Romantic Relationship Melt away old relationships, resentments, patterns and bad habits in order to open your heart to soulful, romantic love. And, if you are single and want a partner, do you believe he or she really exists? If you are coupled, can your current relationship be re-ignited and fulfill you?

Personal Growth, Spirituality & Religion Let your faith and beliefs serve you on a daily basis. Give up the ones that hinder you or no longer align with who you have become.

Fun & Play Don't wait to instill play. Feed your soul by carving out time to play or learn something new. Choose your playmates and playgrounds carefully. Plan the big and small adventures. And don't wait for the "some days…life is short."

Physical Spaces What stuff needs to be thrown away, donated or sold in order to open up space for the things you want in your surroundings. If you do not love your physical backdrops, then what are you holding on to? Can you create a space that is reflective of you?

Author Henry David Thoreau wrote, "Go confidently in the direction of your dreams. Live the life you have imagined." With the New Year upon you, look into your heart and create an exquisite vision that honors you and the enchanting life you want, one that includes richness, fullness, passion and wisdom. Let this new beginning empower you to believe that this time, you will find something extraordinary, witnessing everyday miracles and embracing the reality of a beautiful, blissful life.

Coaching Questions to Empower You:

1. What do you really want?

2. What do your heart and soul long for?

3. What's possible?

4. What will sustain you, and what will stop you?

5. Where can you find magic in your life everyday?

Show Your Affection

February 2011

> "Too often we underestimate the power of a touch, a smile, a kind word, a listening ear, an honest accomplishment, or the smallest act of caring, all of which have the potential to turn a life around."
> Leo Buscaglia

I admit it…I am a romantic at heart. I melt watching people hold hands, exchange sweet glances and give pecks to one another on the cheek. I enjoy seeing couples, young and old, honor their love by showing affection, warmth and kindness to each other. I somehow think it's a reflection of their deeper love by their willingness to reveal their fondness towards each other with a sweet sense of confidence, tenderness and devotion.

When is comes to exploring the topic of public display of affection, or rather "PDA", it seems to me that it can often be misinterpreted. On one hand, I believe in expressing love, embracing intimacy and connecting to your partner in a way that honors not only the individuals but also the relationship itself. Yet, PDA has earned a bad reputation too often when some people cross a line, allow their displays to be inappropriate and do not respect boundaries, theirs and others.

Let's consider the importance of affection. For couples, it can be an expression of love and serves as a reminder to each other that they are connected. For others, it can be sweet gesture that reunites, welcomes or greets someone with respect, kindness and caring. Some people meet their friends and family members with a hug or quick kiss. Consider the customs of individuals in other cultures who perhaps give a kiss on one or both cheeks. Even with strangers, a smile is shared and a hand is extended to someone you first meet, thereby showing affection immediately. The right physical touch, whether in an intimate relationship or new introduction, can create a safe connection, a trusted bond, and the good, warm feelings that are so often desired.

So, what keeps you from fully expressing your own feelings and affections towards others? Do you have an open heart not only to your partner but also others in general? Are you comfortable in your own skin and feel confident about the person you are presenting to the world? If not, you must first feel good about yourself in order to express your true feelings and show your affection genuinely and lovingly towards others. Here are some tips for creating a closeness that will allow affection to be present.

Tips for Creating Affection and Intimacy in Your Relationship:

- Nourish and love yourself first.
- Always be who you are.
- Look good, feel good and be healthy.
- Have impeccable hygiene.
- Cherish your mate unconditionally.
- Love deeply.
- Be generous with others.
- Treasure the relationship itself.
- Disclose your thoughts, dreams, fears, hopes, wants, desires.
- Say what you feel.
- Smile all day.
- Ask for what you need courageously.
- Continually practice compassion and forgiveness.
- Align your words and actions.
- Have an open heart.
- Learn about each other.
- Meet strangers with a handshake.
- Give hugs freely.
- Communicate consistently.
- Know your boundaries.
- Deepen your passion.
- Be bold.
- Reveal your inner self.

When you feel good about whom you are and share yourself with others, a natural friendliness and liking can be extended in all of your relationships. Learning to show affection in a way that is right for you can not only satisfy your soul but also lead you back to your most authentic self.

In this higher purpose, you can open your heart, share your uniqueness and spread your love to others in the world.

A Coaching Exercise to Show Your Affection:

1. Do you love who you are and how you show up in the world?

2. Are there any personal boundaries you need to set, emotionally or physically?

3. With your romantic partner, what is it to love deeply and keep the chemistry alive?

4. With your family, how could your affections break down any barriers and create stronger bonds? How do you express love towards them?

5. With friends, how do you want to honor them with your affections?

6. With new acquaintances, how could a sign of warmth facilitate a new relationship?

7. Smile, hug, kiss, hold hands and love as much as possible.

Recycle Your Best Self

March 2011

> "We define ourselves by the best that is in us, not the worst that has
> been done to us."
> Edward Lewis

As I sat down to write this column, I considered the recycling theme, and many ideas came up… anything from re-tooling past skills for a new job and re-igniting passionate pursuits to re-claiming lost relationships and honoring the vintage in life. But the most important emergence was the thought of recycling yourself in the world as you go through life. Being true to yourself is about re-claiming who you are by constantly being aware of your own values; taking what life brings you and re-assessing along the way; and then trusting yourself to make selective adjustments that still honor you. Being authentic is the ability to reuse the good that exists from within you to make a discerning, positive impact on both yourself and others.

My company, Excavive™ Life Coaching, was created eight years ago as a way to empower people, especially women, to pursue their passions, increase their self-confidence, and build the kind of lives they truly want to live. The key messages I have embraced and promoted in my work have been about evolving and uncovering your authentic self. So, what follows are my most important messages, along with provocative coaching questions to inspire you to be your best under any circumstances. Knowing who you are and how to find your own answers from within based on your deepest, soulful desires is one of the best ways to create an empowered and fulfilling life. So get started now by courageously giving yourself permission to be your best, no matter where your starting point exists.

The Five Most Important "Evolved" Messages to Help You Be Your Best:

1. **Love Yourself First and Know Who You Are** Know your essence and what is important to you. Live your values. Reveal your inner self. Nourish and love yourself first. Take care of you so you can take care of others. Don't betray yourself and always be who you are.

   • Do you love who you are and how you show up in the world?
   • What **unique** values, strengths or skills do you have that directly supports your authenticity? Name at least 3.
   • Are you living in a balanced way that is deeply satisfying and truly expresses you and your soul? (Be sure you are living YOUR life.)
   • Start acting today based on who you want to be tomorrow... how can you be extraordinary now?
   • How can you pamper yourself today?

2. **Pursue Passion NOW** Know what makes you feel alive and consciously follow those activities that help you feel connected to yourself and others. Dance, sing, play, travel, dream, visualize, grow and create. Seek and expand your possibilities. Love being alive, know what you are passionate about, follow your urges, and be wildly happy, there is no time to waste so get going now.

   • What does it feel like to be awed?
   • What activities have heart and soul meaning for you?
   • List five things you truly desire.
   • What is your one unrelenting passion, and are you taking inspired action steps to manifest your reality?

3. **Use Your Voice Powerfully** You are always free to choose your thoughts, beliefs, attitudes and actions so learn to express yourself authentically by communicating clearly, truthfully and positively; exuding confidence; creating connection; and listening actively. Do you know what you REALLY want? Practice wanting. If you ask for what you desire, you might

just get it. Not asking is an automatic no. And, besides, who knows what you want better than yourself. Learn to say yes when you mean yes, no when you mean no. Make your words and actions meet. Set boundaries, Say NO often. Understand the power of silence.

- How are you using your voice to say what you want/need and how you feel?
- Are you being nice or are you being real?
- Count the number of times you speak powerfully each and every day until it becomes a habit.

4. **Practice Gratitude Every Day** Be appreciative, understanding, kind, and compassionate; and express it often. Choose what you have in every moment. Savor your current life and try to see the good every day. Be generous with your heart. Continually practice compassion and forgiveness by having as much empathy for yourself as you do others.

- Who and what are you grateful for today? Start a Gratitude journal, say prayers of thanks, and acknowledge others' generous acts.
- Is there someone you need to acknowledge or be of service to?
- List ALL of your blessings, big and small, by including everyone and everything. Attempt to capture at least 50 things you are grateful for.

5. **Create a LIFE Vision to Go Towards** Create a new vision of what you want, now and going forward. Ask yourself, will these items create a sustainable "essence" of what you want long-term, i.e., greater intimacy with a partner, a more fulfilling career, creative inspiration for a passionate pursuit, or greater compassion for others. Are you following your bliss? Is your work irresistible, meaningful, or important to you? Engage in something that you adore and brings you joy, even if it looks messy or unexplainable to others. Be fierce for it.

- How have you withheld yourself from life?
- What could the best possible future look like?

- What do you really, really, really want?
- How will this item move you forward in reaching your goals and connecting you to your bigger life vision?
- What distractions exist in your life that keeps you from being your authentic self? List the things you do instead of being fabulous. (AND yes, laundry can be included!)
- Do you have people who support your vision, in other words, your "army of advocates?"
- Do you live from the inside out or outside in?
- If everything is possible, what is the next best step towards meeting your BIG goals?

Recycling yourself is about salvaging your goodness, accepting where you are right now and using all of your best qualities to move forward living an authentic life that is blissfully joyful, abundantly balanced, positively impactful and authentically meaningful. This is your great life, so make the most of it now.

Be at Home

April 2011

"Everyone is a house with four rooms: physical, mental, emotional, spiritual. Unless we go into every room every day, even if only to keep it aired, we are not a complete person."

Rumer Godden

This issue marks my 48th column for *Underwired* Magazine, and it is also the month I am getting married to a man from my hometown of Fort Worth, Texas. Having lived in Louisville, Kentucky, for over 20 years, I love the timing of this month's theme, the "Ville" (as in "Louisville") issue, since I have been thinking about home, specifically where I live, work, and play; and the real meaning of not only my physical spaces, but also the people who inhabit those places with me. I live in Kentucky with my teenage children; am adding a Texas home with new family members; and plan to continue to go back and forth to meet the needs of my family and clients. So, when it comes to thinking about " home," I have been pondering the many aspects that make up a home, the real meaning of a home, and what it has to offer not only me but others as well.

For many people, home is defined by the boundaries of their physical space, or, their actual house. Others consider home to be their birthplace, their hometown or the house they grew up in. Several people deem their dwelling to be their current place of residence and the community in which they participate. Some people only feel at home when they are connected to a community; and they have created strong bonds with others by making new friends, getting involved as a citizen or volunteer, joining organizations, clubs and churches or synagogues, enjoying the natural landscapes, discovering the city's cultural opportunities such as the arts, sporting events and great restaurants, and doing meaningful work. And, finally, there are a few who believe they are residents of the world, finding that they are at home wherever they are in any given moment.

So, where do you LIVE? Where do you feel most at home? And if you are lost, exploring or wondering, how do you find your way back to a home base for yourself? Here are some places to start looking….

The Physical Dwelling Your house is the place where you live, your residence. It is the financial investment that is perhaps a mirror of your success and a pay-off your hard work. By caring for the actual home, keeping it clean and clutter free, making improvements and designing it to your tastes, you create the headquarters for your life.

A Reflection of Emotion & Beauty Create a space that is reflective of you and your personal style. The colors, the textures, the scents, the lighting, the art, and the furnishings all set the tone and mood, and can provoke feelings of comfort, inspiration and joy. How do you want to feel in your space? What do you want to express? And, don't forget, the objects within bring meaning, and perhaps history, and allow for the further personalization of your space. Textile designer William Morris said, "Have nothing in your house that you do not know to be useful, or believe to be beautiful."

A Container for Family Your home is the place to create fond memories and build a rich archive for you, your family and friends. The daily routines, the milestone celebrations, the inevitable yet solvable disagreements, the actual caring of the home and its members, the playful moments, the sharing with friends and neighbors, and the safety and security of the house are all important aspects of building a strong home life. And, your parents or other family member's homes can be a place to visit or return to.

A Community Playground Have you experienced the feeling of coming home to familiar people and places by re-uniting with childhood friends or distant family, revisiting your old home or school, or dining at your old favorite standbys that still exist? (Mine is Joe T. Garcia's in Fort Worth.) Can you find connections to a new community by engaging in its cultural offerings, getting involved in a local cause or joining a church? Being grounded in a community allows you to find meaningful experiences and surround yourself with people who have similar values or interests. Being an island can be lonely, but finding a home community can help you strengthen your home base and build a new, empowered sense of family and self.

A Sanctuary for Self And finally, home is always a place you feel content within yourself. Do you feel comfortable in your own skin? "I live in my house as I live inside my skin: I know more beautiful, more ample, more sturdy and more picturesque skins: but it would seem to me unnatural to exchange them for mine, " wrote Italian chemist and writer Primo Levi. To help you find inner peace, create a special space of your own within your home… a place to be quiet, a place to feel nurtured, a place to reflect, a place to breath, a place to feel your heart beat, a place to be your best, a place to be at home.

Coaching Questions to Be at Home:

1. Where is your home?

2. What qualities are important to you about your home… peace, comfort, safety and security? Beauty, family bonding, celebrations, entertaining, and community outreach? Security, business, financial investment, and success?

3. If lost, uneasy or misaligned, how do you find your way back home?

4. Do you feel at home in your home, and does your space reflect you, your distinct flair and your family's personal heritage?

5. How can you create magic, joy and bliss in and out your home everyday?

German Writer Johann Wolfgang Von Goethe said, "Be he a king or a peasant, he is happiest who finds peace at home." And, inspirational writer Sarah Ban Breathnach wrote, "Be grateful for the home you have, knowing that at this moment, all you have is all you need." So, whether you are a transplant to your current town, a homegrown city dweller or you have more than one house, you get to create your home to best reflect who you are based on your personal style, as well as to meet you and your family's needs. But most of all, don't forget that no matter where you are, home is wherever you are. Whether you are coming, going, staying, visiting, moving, shifting- YOUR best home is wherever YOU are.

Capture the Extraordinary, not the Ordinary...
Your Aha Moments

May 2011

"Don't wait for extraordinary opportunities. Seize common occasions and make them great. Weak men wait for opportunities; strong men make them."
Orison Swett Marden

Embracing the Aha's of life... I am thrilled with the subject of discovering revelations, witnessing turning points, capturing ultimate creativity and seeing the shift in real time as it occurs in people's lives. After all, as a Life Coach, I am privy to amazing "aha" moments, big and small, each and every day- mine, friends, clients- and I see magic take hold as the miracles occur. So, I thought this subject would be easy to write about. But when it came down to actually putting on paper what I believe to be important, it became rather challenging. How do you explain these amazing events, the marvel...the wonder...the awe.... the vision?

I started thinking about the many times I have seen my clients "get it," as well as had my own experiences with growth and evolvement, and I realized that there are consistencies with the "what," "when" and "how" these revelations occur. These moments of clarity can be about yourself, anything or any situation. For instance, many times the extraordinary is found in the ordinary moments of life. Have you ever had the perfect idea come to you when you are driving, showering, cleaning or exercising? I call these moments "out of mind" experiences. When you let go, relax and stop thinking about it, sometimes the answers come quickly.

Another way the light bulb goes off is by getting quiet through meditation, resting, journaling and listening to the small voice inside. Inventor Thomas Edison said, "When you become quiet, it just dawns on you." This intuition is the part of self that knows the inner truth. When I attended my first life coaching training almost eight years ago, one of the first things I learned is that everyone is "creative, resourceful and whole; and they have their answers inside themselves." I understood that people were fully capable but what I did not recognize at the time is how powerful and provocative tapping into one's inner source could be in realizing the important matters of life. There is unlimited power and potential in realizing one's own destiny, rather than having someone else tell you what to do or how to be.

So, when does the desire to do it differently and go into the unknown become more compelling than staying stuck and reaping the same results? What makes someone want to search for new answers and make sustainable life changes? I believe either the pain becomes too great that the payoff no longer has value... or the vision becomes so clear that you can no longer ignore it. And sometimes, the combination of both fear and foresight gets someone moving.

No matter what your reason is for change, what is important is that you do not stay stagnate, sell yourself short or allow your blocks to hold you back. Be true to yourself and find your enlightened path by tapping into your values, vision and purpose. Become aware of your desires, accept all aspects of yourself and take action to revitalize your life. Start asking the *right* questions so that you will know what is best for you. Let's get started....

Powerful Coaching Questions to Help You Reach Your "Aha" Moments:

Self-discovery is an enlightening process; and you can excavate your true desires, core beliefs and best course of action by going within and getting truly curious. From the list below, I suggest choosing the questions that best speak to you in each progressive area of Awareness, Acceptance and Action. You are powerful, innovative, all knowing and imaginative and I believe your answers are within yourself. So get started. Ask yourself what you REALLY want, accept your current circumstances and then find fearless fierceness and bold courage to move forward.

"Ah-wareness"

1. Are you living in a way that is deeply satisfying and truly expresses you and your soul?

2. When was the last time you experienced true wonder? Describe the peak experiences that have made you the happiest, and look for any common themes.

3. What do you want more of?

4. What is enticing and tantalizing enough to take big risks for your own happiness?

5. When you want blissful solitude, what are your uninterrupted escapes that allow you to feel happy and peaceful?

6. What does it feel like to be awed?

7. What is the ONE thing you always think of that makes you smile?

8. Do you live from the inside out, or outside in?

9. What inspires you?

10. What is it to be generous with yourself?

11. What is it to have a full, rich life?

12. What thrills you?

"Ah-cceptance"

1. Who are you becoming?

2. How have you withheld yourself from life?

3. How can you be extraordinary now?

4. Define what you want, now and later. Do you have an inspiring life vision that includes, fun, happiness and meaning?

5. What does your heart say?

6. How do you want to transcend?

7. Where can you find magic in your life everyday?

8. What have you built and what is your legacy?

"Ah-ction"

1. Get clear... are your goals compelling enough to take bold action? Will they create stunning success and marvelous joy?

2. What are you giving up by not taking inspired action NOW?

3. Will doing THIS bring you joy?

4. Describe your perfect day, week or month.

5. What could the best possible future look like?

6. If everything is possible, what is the next step towards achieving your dreams?

7. Powerfully interpret your current situation, and decide what you are going to do to "get going?" If you were at your best, what would you do next, and go do that.

8. What do you want to complete?

When you begin to recognize the things in your life that inspire you and release what is not working, then you will begin to move more rapidly toward those surprising moments. By using your intuitive intelligence, creative thinking and rational reasoning, you will open yourself to sudden moments of understanding, clearer paths and your deepest desires realized. Listen up and capture the extraordinary... your Aha moments await.

Be Truly Powerful with Work You Love

June 2011

> "It is the soul's duty to be loyal to its own desires. It must abandon itself to its master passion."
> Rebecca West

Do you love your job? No kidding- do you really, really, really enjoy what you do? Do you wake up each day ready to embrace the opportunity to shine? Or, are you filled with dread and lack of motivation? Do you feel satisfied with your rewards and your contributions, or do you just get by, hoping that things will be different tomorrow?

Working is part of life, and for most people, it provides a way for people to take care of themselves and their families. It is also where people spend the majority of their waking hours. A large number of my coaching clients come to me because they are unfulfilled in their careers. So, it is interesting to me as a Life Coach that so many people are so unhappy with what they do, yet stay so long. I often ask, "If you do not love what you do, then why do you do what you do?" The reasons vary: to provide for themselves and their families; to have a certain lifestyle; to use their education, skills and training; to feel useful and make a contribution; to help others; to use their creativity; to support other passions, to invest in their future. People also stay in jobs because they feel stuck in a job, do not have the confidence or courage to change, or simply do not know what they really want to do. Where do you fall?

I believe it is important to enjoy what you do and if you do not, then you need to get fierce to find happiness in your work. You matter and your work matters, and people everywhere are longing for meaningful work where they are compensated for their full value. Many people find most of their self-worth in their work, and when it is off-track, self-esteem suffers. Although I do not believe what you do solely defines you, finding the right fit can create a stronger sense of self and greater understanding of how you fit into a bigger picture of your life and the world. A person's work can play a large role in fulfilling a life purpose with meaning, passion and joy. So, whether you stay at home with children, work in an office, are on the road, volunteer or are retired, it is not only vital to get your own needs met, but also to share your strengths, wisdom and gifts with others so that they can benefit from your brilliance. Imagine... what would it be like to fully show up at your work- strong, powerful and excited about what you are doing, really be happy with your accomplishments, synergize those around you to also be their best and then be rewarded for a job well done that you actually enjoy?

No matter where you are in your work cycle, I believe you can find joy in what you do every day by understanding yourself first, deciding what you want to do, boldly positioning yourself for your best fit and then choosing how you want to show up for not only your calling but also your life. It is up to you to determine your best career path as well as choose how you want to show up each and every day... strong or weak, engaged or detached, helpful or hurtful, excited or depressed? Love what you do and get the most out of your profession, whether you are in transition or have your dream job. Regardless, of where you are on your career path, here are some ways to be strong and confident for your work each and every day.

Tips on Being Your Authentic Best at Work:

- Know yourself first and be real.
- Live a balanced life.
- Love what you do.
- Use your assets, strengths and values at work.
- Bring your heart to work with you.
- Make meaning in what you do, in both the big and small things. Be grateful.
- Understand how you fit into the big picture.
- Understand your personal impact and circle of influence.
- Be in integrity by doing what you say you will do.
- Use your voice.
- Dress and act the part, be professional.
- Have down time.
- Find a mentor and your personal professional advocates.

- Create a personal vision and personal growth plan for your work.
- Be present and engaged while you are there.
- Be creative.
- Ask for feedback.
- Learn what you do not know and ask for help, communicate clearly.
- Get paid what you are worth.
- Use ALL of your vacation time and take advantage of your benefits.
- Stay out of office drama and gossip.
- Don't be a victim to a job you think you are supposed to keep.
- Play nice, learn to get along and build bridges with the others. Listen.
- Create a feedback loop for validation- most people want to be appreciated and recognized for their hard work.
- Create an exit strategy if it is not working for you.

Engaging in what you love to do and fully expressing that with courage ignites enthusiasm. Being contagiously passionate and authentically engaged raises the bar for everyone else and positively impacts the people around you. I hope you actually like what you do. In fact, I want you to adore what you do each and every day… because when you are at your best, it feels like play and everyone benefits. Confucius said, "Choose a job you love, and you will never have to work a day in your life." Are you ready?

Powerful Coaching Questions:

1. Do you adore your work?
2. If not, what's missing?
3. How do you show up at work?
4. Are you "you" while doing what you do?
5. If not, what would make it congruent?
6. What are three steps you could take immediately to either find more satisfaction in your current role, or begin to discover what's next?

Pop-Up: Make Your Life 3-Dimensional

July 2011

> "If we did all the things we are capable of, we would literally astound ourselves."
> Thomas Edison

In considering this month's "Pop" theme, at first I entertained the idea of writing about pop culture and the impact it has on individuals. After all, it is easy to get swept up in the current trend of what is popular and acceptable. And, my point would be to fight for your individuality, to know thyself and be true to your own essence, despite what is being thrown at you from the media and other cultural avenues. However, it seemed like it was the same message I convey over and over again, and if you have read my previous columns or have worked with me as your Life Coach, you know I consistently promote being authentic and real. An important message, but also a bit flat, tired and boring. So what if there is more than just "being yourself." What if you could be the true you AND have the great, fulfilling life by being bolder, more colorful, and more playful while constantly learning, growing, evolving and expanding. Being real and bigger at the same time.

My message to you is like a greeting card… one that says, "I acknowledge you; I honor you; I am thinking of you; I recognize your achievements; I love you; I wish you well. But at the same time, I want to hugely celebrate you and encourage you to go for your dreams. Embrace your bigness and don't waste a single moment." Instead of a flat card that opens up with an inspirational message, I am sending you a "pop-up" 3-D card… one that is more creative, surprising, vivid and unexpected, and gives more dimension to who you are. Don't just mark the events of your life with store-bought, trite, status quo sayings, but create your own visionary pop-up that jumps out and says to the world, I am fully here.

Is your life like a traditional one-sided greeting card that is collapsed, boring and only presents a single point of view… or are you like a three-dimensional pop-up card that is surprisingly playful, fearlessly courageous and makes a more striking statement? Here are some thoughts and life perspectives to consider while bursting out of the ordinary into an extraordinary, bigger you in the world…

8 Elements of a "Pop-Up" to Embrace and Integrate into Your Life:

1. **Unexpected & Surprising** When you open a card and a pop-up jumps off the page, the element of surprise is usually present. Let your life be spontaneous, bewildering and astonishing. Learn to be open to new, unexpected, dazzling and, possibly, uncomfortable experiences. You never know when you will be amazingly awed.

2. **Colorful** Pop-ups are unique, artful and vibrant. Engage in many adventures so that your life is bright, vivid and colorful. Honor your individuality.

3. **Meaningful** When someone gives a card, the intent is to express a thought and honor the other person; to make it mean something. Do you find significance in the things you do? Are your life's actions creating a profound and positive impact in the world? Find your life purpose.

4. **Fun & Playful** Laugh, seek humor and have joy in your life. Are you having fun in the day-to-day; AND are you pursuing enjoyable, passion-driven hobbies or activities? You can never have too much fun.

5. **Contained** A pop-up grows taller, but stays in its space. Have boundaries that protect your emotional and physical space. Honor your personal values and don't let others define you.

6. **Expansive** A standard greeting card can be flat, dull and lackluster. A pop-up expands upward and is no longer limited to the original space provided. Elevate your own playing field by acknowledging your own current limitations and then

embracing limitless possibilities for your personal growth, lifelong learning and unending expansion. Start with your dreams and desires and then build upwards.

7. **New Perspectives** Taking an image from a level surface to 3-dimensional form gives the viewer new ways to see the same thing. Take a current life issue and think of the many different perspectives awaiting you. Perhaps you can look at something from your boss', spouse's, friend's or even children's viewpoint. Learn to ask different questions, get curious and respect other people's opinions. Expand your scope and you might learn something enriching and new.

8. **Lifelike** Seeing something effervesce, jump off the page and come alive can make it more believable, more real, and more exciting. Fill-in the intricate details and find your own sparkly authenticity.

Whatever "pop-up" elements you choose to apply to your life, create a vision that is deliberate, inspiring, playful, balanced, expansive and will move you into action. Holy Man Black Elk said, "A vision without a task is a dream. A task without a dream is drudgery. But a vision with a task can change the world." Give yourself the gift of new perspectives... start with the space you have and then grow taller. Use your vivid imagination to boldly pop out to be the unique and wonderful you.

Popping the Right Questions:

1. If you could do anything, what are the possibilities? Think big and tall.

2. If your dreams, desires and life vision were created on a pop-up, what would you reflect?

- What images would you use?
- What story or message would you reveal?
- What objects or people need to be included?

3. How can you have your life be a fun celebration that is a true reflection of you?

4. Where do you hold back or stop short?

5. How can you double, even triple, your vitality?

6. What is the new elevation from which you want to regard your life?

Choose Intentionally: Your Money, Your Time & Your Energy

August 2011

> "Life begets life. Energy creates energy. It is by spending oneself that one becomes rich."
> Sarah Bernhardt

Do you have a budget- a way to allot your resources for a given period of time? Does your plan line up with your inspired goals, authentic values, true desires and expansive dreams- or do you stay stuck in survival mode, just trying to make it and hoping it will all work out? When you hear the word, "budget" do you get excited knowing you have a plan in place and feel positively confident that you make strong choices? Or, does the idea of a budget make you cringe with the negative thoughts of fear, guilt, doubt and uncertainty, making you feel like you are being held back, restricted or put in a box?

Discussions about how time and money are spent are everywhere, and for most people, it conjures up mixed reactions, good and bad. Many people are financially savvy, yet might be challenged with how they manage their time. For example, they work hard and make plenty of money yet they don't indulge in the things that bring them joy such as playtime, downtime, enough time with people they love or even fully using their vacation time. Others might be efficient with their time, and but lack the resources or the confidence to create more abundance in their relationship with money, and thus feel vulnerable in life.

So when it comes to truly maximizing your resources, a budget serves the purpose of creating a foundation to best utilize all of your resources to live a rich life full of meaningful experiences and daily mastery. It's the paradox of expansiveness-— restricting what you have in order to better direct it and ultimately increase it. Time and money are the two most common commodities to be sorted and intentionally focused to support what you truly want. But I also believe energy needs to be included in the formula for success. By getting your time and money handled easily, it will increase your vitality and free you up to do what is really needed. So, deliberately allocate not only your money and time, but also your energy. Here are some additional thoughts on purposefully directing your assets.

Intentional Budgeting of Your Resources:

Money What does money do for you? Money can provide security, stability, self-care, learning, adventure, philanthropy, validation, a solid future and a record of success. Your money choices can create either lasting satisfaction or instant gratification. Be in integrity, be generous and be smart with your currency. Although money is an exchange and measure of value, don't let money define your personal value or self-worth, but see it as an empowered energy to use wisely.

- What would you do with unlimited money?
- Does the way you spend your money align with your values?
- Do you include giving back and supporting your causes as part of your financial plan?
- What do you need to financially clean up - debts, overspending, planning, money leaks?
- Do you allocate dream money as part of your budget, allowing you to spend your money pursuing your goals?

Time Do you use your time wisely? It seems everyone complains about not having enough time, when in actuality, I believe it is how time is prioritized. Choose what is really important, be realistic about the undertaking and learn to break down greater endeavors into smaller increments. One way to think about time is to realize that every time you say yes to do something, you are saying no to something else, and vice versa. Decide who and what you will say yes to and who and what you will say no to.

- What would you do with more time?
- Does the way you spend your time match your values and goals?
- Is your deadline real, or did you make it up? Are there other resources are available so you can delegate?
- Do you have life balance?

Energy When you think about the many aspects of your life, energy is exerted for everything that you not only execute but also even think about doing. Eventually- mental, physical and even emotional exhaustion can set in if you are not being true to yourself. In order to re-energize yourself, it is important to identify who or what gives you energy, and who or what takes it away. By identifying the positive and negative influences, you can create more awareness of where the specific "leaks" exist; and then work to re-calibrate your time, energy and resources.

- Do you have enough energy to pursue your passions?
- Do you expend your energy honoring your values and goals?
- Do you protect your energy from the things that drain you, as well as invest in the people, places and things that give you energy?
- How can you double your vitality?

So, what's the point of it all? When you clarify your goals and remove financial barriers, time limitations and energy drains, you can then channel your energy into moving forward and expanding your possibilities of fulfillment. As author Terry McMillan said, "Too many of us are hung up on what we don't have, can't have, or won't ever have. We spend too much energy being down, when we could use that same energy - if not less of it - doing, or at least trying to do, some of the things we really want to do." Start by truthfully assessing where you really are, right-sizing your expectations, getting out of the "some days," creating an intentional living plan, and then fiercely pursue all that you want and desire.

A Coaching Exercise to Re-claim Your Resources and Direct Your Energy:

Using a blank piece of paper, create two columns of the following:

> A "Good" for YOU list
> Who or what gives you energy; creates happiness and wellness; makes you come alive? List all of the people, places and things that bring you pleasure and add to your life. (ex: friends, eating healthy, exercise, time off, daily fresh air, fulfilling work, adventures, self-care, your assets)

> A "Bad" for YOU list
> Who or what drains your energy? What are you tolerating? Who are your "energy vampires?" List everything that irritates

you and is detrimental, big and small, to your wellbeing. (ex: clutter, needy people, perfectionism, not using your voice, fear, skipping meals, your debts)

With the above information, begin to rid yourself (or set boundaries and limits) of the things that do not serve you. Identify the most draining energy zappers and work to eliminate those first, while continuing to make time for the things the nurture you. Budget your energy towards increasing your abundance, your vitality and your overall life satisfaction.

(See "Excavating Your Energy" coaching exercise in the Appendix.)

Claim Your Success

September 2011

> "Try not to become a man of success, but rather try to become a man
> of value."
>
> Albert Einstein

Are you successful, and if so, in what ways? Are you happy with who
you are and what you have achieved? Most often, success is defined by
one's accomplishments—favorable endeavors that come to fruition, the
attainment of wealth, position or honors, or a person who has achieved
success. This description might be true for you, but I also believe the
definition of success must include the "who you are" part; and everyone
must create their own personal definition of success.

So what does success mean to you? How do you define it, claim it and
pursue it? Is it a plentiful bank account, a certain social status, the right
home in the right neighborhood, a title at work, or an educational degree?
Is it your own happiness, the quality of your relationships or a balanced
life? How do you know when you have made it to the top, truly arrived at
your destination, or reached your pinnacle?

Some people feel accomplished professionally. They have mastered their
vocation, are recognized by their peers as an expert, have been rewarded
financially and continue to find success in their work. Their self-esteem is
tied to their career, yet other parts of their life may have suffered. Other
people believe they have done well personally by taking care of their
relationships, their health, their families–fulfilling the role of caretaker,
yet carry a constant disappoint that they have not done enough, achieved
enough, or accumulated enough. Either way, success is being determined
by what they do, not necessarily who they are as a person.

The key to success starts with creating your own personal definition
of achievement that authentically aligns both worlds. Most people need a
combination of both personal and professional victories, while maintaining

life balance, personal connection, shared intimacy through vulnerability, joyful accomplishments, service opportunities and true authenticity to one's life purpose and passionate pursuits. The "being-ness" can be distinguished by your values, a strong sense of self, and seeing the good that already exists within you. The "doing-ness" can be defined by acknowledging what you have already accomplished and what you still have yet to do. Personal success is created by making choices that honor you while continually moving forward to reach your dreams and goals… and in the process, not betraying yourself along the way.

5 Keys to "Being" Successful:

1. **Get Passionate** What excites you? Is there anything you are so bothered by that you can't you not do? Get inspired, dream big, pursue passion, and love what you do. Envision your achievements, engage in creative solutions, and be boldly brave. "Success isn't a result of spontaneous combustion. You must set yourself on fire," shared Humorist Arnold Glasgow.

2. **Get Confident** Believe in your personal ability to succeed. Be fearless and adventurous; take risks and dare to succeed. Lead your efforts with self-confidence and unshakable certainty. Women's rights activist and novelist Lydia M. Child said, "Belief in oneself is one of the most important bricks in building any successful venture." If you do not believe in you, how can you expect others to do the same?

3. **Get Clear** Intentionally choose what you want and remain authentic to your self on the journey. Decide what is right for you based on all life areas —emotionally, physically, mentally, financially, relationally and socially. "Right-size" your expectations, especially of yourself and others. Realistically, what can you do now? Maximize your time, talent and resources. British journalist David Frost said, "Don't aim for success if you want it; just do what you love and believe in, and it will come naturally."

4. **Get Empowered** Artist Pablo Picasso said, "Action is the foundational key to all success." Take inspired action everyday. Be grateful for your accomplishments and learn from your

failures. And no matter what, keep moving forward. Do something, anything towards your goals and do not waste a moment not pursuing your dreams.

5. **Get Supported** Ask for help... know when, know who and know how. Encourage feedback, make new decisions and learn from everything. Evaluate if what you are doing is effective and re-calibrate as needed. Remember, you are always in choice. As French philosopher Albert Camus said, "Life is the sum of all your choices."

5 Easy Steps to Attaining Success:

1. **Define your goal or objective.** Set soulful goals that reflect who you are and the impact you want to make. See the end result and work backwards.

2. **Create a plan** with inspired action steps and a realistic timetable to achieve that success. Pick three things each day to work towards your aspirations.

3. **Follow your path.** Be purposeful, stay on track and do not waste time, money or energy.

4. **Re-evaluate and adjust the plan along the way.** Get feedback and make sure what you are doing is working. Remember the definition of insanity is doing the same thing over and over again, and expecting different results.

5. **See the success.** Did you meet your own personal expectations? Was the pursuit of that goal to your highest capacity? Did you do your best, no matter the outcome? Savor your success and then ask, "What is next?"

The combination of "being" and "doing" is met with how you handle the ups and downs along the way. By doing the best you can in any given moment with the knowledge and resources on hand, you can build a strong foundation for continued success in any given situation. Here are some provocative inquiries to see if you are on your path to triumph.

5 Thoughtful Coaching Questions to Move You Towards Success:

1. What would true success look like to you, and what would that get you?

2. What kind of plan do you need to create to get there? What resources are available to you, and how will you be supported?

3. How do you suppose you could change your current situation to better reflect your desired situation?

4. If your whole attention is focused on producing this result, what will you have to give up? Do you need to re-calibrate and if so, where do you go from here?

5. What is your contribution to the world going to be? Is this your desired legacy?

Conclusion

"There is more in us than we know. If we can be made to see it,
perhaps, for the rest of our lives, we will be unwilling to settle for less."
Kurt Hahn

The True You is meant to be a catalyst to *excavate* who you really are; to *explore* the depths of your own greatness while discovering how it matches your dreams and desires; then to *evolve* into the best version of yourself, fully living the life you want. None of this information will serve you if you do not integrate the learning and tools you have uncovered along this journey- and begin to take authentically inspired action.

My hope for you is that you will find outrageous courage; deep inner strength and unstoppable determination to not only embrace *The True You*, but to live your truest life every day in every way possible. Russian writer Leo Tolstoy said, "True life is lived when tiny changes occur."

So I ask you, what are you waiting for? There is no time to waste living your most fabulous life. Visit *The True You* often. And if you are unable to move forward on your own, I hope you will consider investing in your own fantastically supportive Life Coach.

And finally, I would love to hear about your success stories on how you have reconnected to your true self: big or small, easy or hard, with beautiful grace or messy chaos… they are all part of the big story of your life. Feel free to e-mail me- your joys, your sorrows, your celebrations, your life experiences at jennifer@excavive.com.

Appendix

Excavating Your Thoughts:
Journaling to Your Authentic Self

A journal is a private place to record your inner thoughts, feelings, "ah ha" moments and desires. Journaling is a form of self-expression, healing, learning, prayer, meditation and creation; it is an illustration of your personality and your innermost being. The more you write, the more you will gain a better understanding of who you are and what you want your life to look like.

Albert Clayton Gaulden, founder and director of The Sedona Intensive, requires his clients to journal as part of his five-day Intensive Clearing program. He states, "Writing your way out of a bad place is the surest way to leave room for the good things in life. My clients keep daily diaries or journals as a way to check in with themselves. It is the retro brilliance of therapy today. I recommend that everyone keep one--beginning with 6-year-olds!"

Your journal is your most trusted keeper of your life's history—it will become your archive. It is a place to record your deepest feelings, darkest secrets, hidden emotions, greatest joys, biggest fears, and longings for what you want in your life. The more you write, the more you will know about yourself. Dream, desire, discover, let go, and love.

Some of the benefits of journaling include...

1. **Learning about Yourself**

   Journaling gives you a deeper connection to who you are as a person and gives you insights to know what you want to do with your life—a brilliant avenue for self-discovery.

2. **Enhancing your Self-Care**

   Consistent writing causes you to stop and think about yourself. Get to know what you need to do for yourself to stay happy and healthy…spiritually, mentally, emotionally and physically.

3. **Increasing Self-Confidence**

   Recording your life helps give you courage to pursue your passions and validation to see the power in taking steps toward what you want.

4. **Setting Goals**

   Writing about your goals and seeing the progress you make helps to monitor how well you are achieving them.

5. **Relieving Stress**

   Writing helps you to release your inner thoughts, fears, frustrations and anger. It gets the stress out of your body.

6. **Letting Go of the Past**

   Journaling will often bring up unresolved issues. It can be an exercise to unearth what needs to be cleaned out or de-cluttered so that there is room for the new experiences, people or things you want in your life.

7. **Experiencing Serenity**

   Peace and calm is often reached through the process of writing. Many people use their journal as a tool to assist in prayer and meditation.

How do you get started?

Find a comfortable spot, a place where you feel safe, loved and inspired. It can be a favorite chair, your bed, a fun coffee shop—any place where you are free to let your mind go. Make a cup of tea. Light a candle. Set the mood. Go to the park and throw down a blanket. Take yourself to your favorite restaurant and write while you wait for your food. Carry your journal with you and write when you are inspired.

Clear you mind, relax, and let your thoughts flow freely. Be sure to record the date, and if you want, the time and place. Do not censor anything, and do not worry about punctuation, grammar, spelling or anything else. Do not edit but draw, doodle and write—let it flow.

Anything that comes out is right. Do not judge your thoughts or feelings; they are YOURS, there are no rights or wrongs.

How often do you write?

Whenever, wherever you want. Your journal is there for you when you feel like writing or reflecting about anything. Preferably, I suggest several times per week for consistency and rhythm. In the morning it can set a mood or intention for the day (It is not a "to do" list, however.) At the end of the day, it can be a clearinghouse to release or bring closure to any issues so you can prepare for a solid night's sleep.

A Word of Caution...

Don't leave your journal in a place where others can read it—protect yourself so you are free to express yourself. Also, never write anger letters to others in your journal. If you need to release your anger through writing, use a separate piece of paper so you can dispose of it in the way that feels best to you.

Now that you are ready, some suggestions on what to write:

1. **Answer a Powerful Question**

   The list below will inspire the flow of words and thoughts.

2. **Name your Feelings**

   What caused the feeling, what were you doing at the time you were triggered? What can you learn about yourself in this moment?

3. **Get Inspired**

   Refer to a daily thoughts book, any inspirational book, a book of quotes, or the Bible or other spiritual book. Write about the thought for the day, or simply open the book and see what presents itself to you.

4. **Use Affirmations**

   These present-tense statements set an intention about how you want your life to be. Always write them as "I am" statements. Ex: "I am a safe in all of my relationships, and I give and receive lots of love." In her book, *I Can Do It,* Louise L. Hay writes, "An affirmation opens the door. It's the beginning point on the path to change. In essence, you're saying to your subconscious mind: *I am taking responsibility. I am aware that there is something to change.* When I talk about doing affirmations, I mean consciously choosing the words that will either help you eliminate something from your life or help create something new in your life."

5. **Express Gratitude**

   Knowing for whom and what you are grateful is very powerful.

6. **Capture Dreams**

   Write about your dreams, either when you first awaken in the morning and remember something from the night before, or daydream about new vision of what you long for.

7. **Set Goals**

   Write a goal that brings out a child-like excitement, one that you can really imagine. Fully describe it by seeing it, touching it, smelling it, feeling it, hearing it.

8. **Record Your Experiences**

   Describe what gives you strength or challenges you to grow. Write how you have persevered and overcome obstacles.

9. **Draw or Doodle**

   Use color to reflect your mood. Cut out photos or pictures. Don't be limited by words. Be creative and have fun.

Questions to inspire...

What are you feeling right now? *(Sample feelings: happy, sad, shy, excited, sorry, proud, embarrassed, angry, guilty, surprised, afraid, impatient, jealous, hopeful, hurt, loved)*

Describe your FAVORITES, and how they inspire you. *(Some fun ideas: color, season, person, holiday, time of day, book, trip, hobby, place, friend, ritual, trait about yourself, accomplishments)*

What is the *next best step* you could take in your life right now?

How would you describe yourself to someone who does not know you?

Make a list of what you are grateful for...Smile.

Describe your perfect day.

Who supports you in your life? Who doesn't?

What excites you and makes you feel alive?

What is your soul's deepest desire?

Is there something from any point in the past you wish you could take back or do over to make it right? How did it feel, then and now?

What are you most afraid of?

What new thing would you love to learn or experience?

Find a special photo or an image. What are your thoughts about what you see?

How do you like to celebrate your birthday and/or your anniversary?

If time and money were of no concern, describe the things you long to do. What do you crave?

What's missing in your life?

Is there a secret you have always wanted to tell, but were afraid?

What do you believe about God? Spirituality? Religion? Higher Power? And, how do you use your beliefs in your everyday life?

What are your unique gifts and talents?

What concerns you about the world, and what would you like to do about it if you could do anything?

List your passions.

What do you want people to say about you?

Do you live your life according to what is most important to you?

What do you value most?

Permission Slip

PERMISSION SLIP

I give myself permission to:

What _____

_____

_____

When _____

_____

_____

With Whom _____

_____

_____

Signature _____

Excavive

UNCOVERING YOUR AUTHENTIC SELF

Jennifer M. Blair
Life Coach ◦ Speaker ◦ Writer
502.893.9589
www.excavive.com
jennifer@excavive.com

©2010

Excavating Your Energy

When you think about the many aspects of your life, energy is exerted for everything that you not only execute but even think about doing. Eventually- mental, physical and even emotional exhaustion can set in. In order to re-energize yourself, it is important to identify who or what gives you energy, and who or what takes it away. By using the list below, you can create awareness of where the specific "leaks" exist; and then work to recalibrate your time, energy and resources.

Date: _____

"Good" for YOU

Who or what gives you energy, creates happiness and wellness, makes you come alive? List all of the people, places and things that bring you pleasure and add to your life. *Examples: friends, eating regularly, exercise, time off, massages, daily fresh air.*

1. _____
2. _____
3. _____
4. _____
5. _____
6. _____
7. _____
8. _____
9. _____
10. _____

"Bad" for YOU

Who or what drains your energy? What are you tolerating? Who are your "energy vampires?" List everything that irritates you and is detrimental to your well being. *Examples: clutter, needy people, perfectionism, not using your voice, skipping meals.*

1. _____
2. _____
3. _____
4. _____
5. _____
6. _____
7. _____
8. _____
9. _____
10. _____

With the above information, begin to rid yourself (or set realistic boundaries) of the things that do not serve you. Identify the most draining energy zappers, and work to eliminate those first, while continuing to make time for the things that nurture you. Take it one item at a time

Excavating Your Accomplishments

Pick a start date and record what you have accomplished so far. What have you achieved recently? What are you proud of or feel good about? To help uncover these endeavors, look at any place where you invest your time, money and effort. Consider both the external and internal you, and look not only to what you have done, but also who you have become.

Start Date: _____

Career:
1.
2.
3.

Community:
1.
2.
3..

Personal growth:
1.
2.
3.

Fun/New Hobbies:
1.
2.
3.

Wellness:
1.
2.
3.

Finances:
1.
2.
3.

Relationships:
1.
2.
3.

Home:
1.
2.
3.

Completion Date: _____

Excavating Your Gratitude

What are you grateful for today? List ALL of your blessings, big and small, and include everyone and everything. Claim the positive changes you have made in your life to this point. Keep this list close by, refer to it often, and add to it as you continue your journey. There is nothing like a dose of gratitude to strengthen your spirit and embrace a more optimistic outlook.

1.	21.
2.	22.
3.	23.
4.	24.
5.	25.
6.	26.
7.	27.
8.	28.
9.	29.
10.	30.
11.	31
12.	32.
13.	33.
14.	34.
15.	35.
16.	36.
17.	37.
18.	38.
19.	39.
20.	40.

Date: _____

Brain Dumping

What's on your mind, occupies your thinking or is bothering you? List all of your thoughts, feelings, ideas, viewpoints, inspirations, dreams, "to do's"... anything that comes to mind. Don't filter or judge as you let your mind wander and thoughts flow. Capture it all as you unload as much as possible.

Date: _____

Either put this list away, trusting that the important things will be accomplished instinctively; or deliberately take inspired action, working on one item at a time. Ask yourself, "What is the next best step, every step of the way?"

Wheel of Life

How satisfied are you in each of these areas of your life...right NOW, _____? (today's date)

The 8 sections in the Wheel of Life represent the areas in your life that support an integrated, balanced and interconnected life. Seeing the center of the wheel as 0 and the outer edge as 10, rank your level of satisfaction in each area of your life by drawing a line to create a new outer edge within the wheel (see sample).

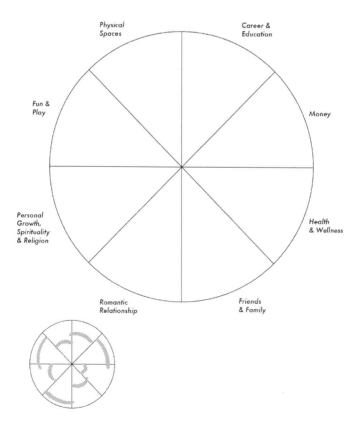

A Sampling of Emotions

Accepted	Ecstatic	Loved
Admired	Elated	Negative
Affectionate	Embarrassed	Nervous
Amazed	Empathetic	Optimistic
Amused	Enraged	Overwhelmed
Angry	Envious	Pleasure
Annoyed	Excited	Positive
Anticipation	Exhausted	Powerful
Anxious	Fearful	Powerless
Ashamed	Friendliness	Proud
Awed	Frustrated	Relaxed
Blissful	Grief	Relieved
Bored	Guilty	Remorse
Calm	Happy	Sad
Cautious	Helpless	Satisfied
Concerned	Hopeful	Serene
Confident	Hopeless	Shame
Confused	Hurt	Shocked
Contempt	Impatient	Shy
Content	Impressed	Stressed
Courageous	Inspired	Surprised
Delighted	Interested	Tension
Depressed	Irritated	Thankful
Despair	Jealous	Tired
Disappointed	Joyful	Trustful
Disgusted	Loathing	Vigilance
Distracted	Lonely	Worried
Doubt	Longing	Zest

Excavating Your Needs

Getting needs met can be a tricky thing. As humans, we have wants and desires, but often don't properly identify what's really missing or needed. In order to start living more authentically and joyfully, you must name it, claim it and take action. Consider what "needs" you currently have relationally, emotionally, spiritually, financially and physically. Listed below are the more prevalent needs I have observed in my coaching practice.

What do you need to be happy and fulfilled?

Some Common Needs:
To be valued, recognized, validated
To be appreciated
To be loved or cherished, adored, treasured, supported, approved of, acknowledged, cared for, accepted unconditionally, saved, rescued
To be included, to belong, to feel part of
To be liked
To be certain, sure, confident, positive
To be comfortable, nurtured
To be free, independent, self-reliant
To be noticed, remembered, seen
To be of service, a leader, a follower
To be trusted
To be heard, listened to
To feel important, needed, useful, busy
To feel connected to others, to a Higher Power, to yourself
To feel safe, secure, protected, stable
To have beauty, order, consistency, perfection
To have peace, calm, quiet, stillness, balance
To have power, strength, influence, acclaim, control
To have abundance, security, stability
To have a cause, vocation, higher purpose
To have honesty, sincerity, loyalty, authenticity, integrity
To have fun, laughter, joy

To have passion, play, pleasure
To have companionship
To have physical touch or connection

1. **Using the above list, identify the three most important needs you currently want fulfilled, rank them in order of importance to you.**

   1. _____
   2. _____
   3. _____

2. **Find three possible creative ways to get each need met.**

   1. _____
   2. _____
   3. _____

3. **Finally, enlist four different people to meet each need for the next month. Overdo it! It is your responsibility to get your own needs met, so ask for what you need. And don't forget to include yourself on this list.**

   1. _____
   2. _____
   3. _____
   4. _____

A Sampling of Values

Achievement	Fun	Personal Power
Accomplishment	Growth	Play
Acknowledgment	Happiness	Present Momentness
Adventure	Harmony	Power
Authenticity	Honesty	Romance
Balance	Honor	Recognition
Beauty	Humor	Respect
Belonging	Independence	Responsibility
Collaboration	Impacting Others	Safety
Community	Inspiration	Self-acceptance
Competition	Integrity	Self-care
Camaraderie	Intensity	Self-expression
Connectedness	Joy	Self-love
Contribution	Learning	Service
Creativity	Loyalty	Spirituality
Directness	Love	Strength
Elegance	Nature	Stylish
Empowerment	Nurturing	Success
Excellence	Order	Tradition
Experiencing	Partnership	Trust
Fairness	Participation	Validation
Flow	Passion	Vitality
Freedom	Peace	
Friends	Performance	

Yes, No and Maybe List

Are you trying to make a decision, get organized and prioritize? Are you feeling overwhelmed, finding it difficult to make decisions on what's next? "Yes, No & Maybe" is an exercise in making proactive choices. Every time you say yes to something, you are saying no to something else. "Yesses" are the must haves. "Nos" can mean not at all, or just not now. And, the "maybes" are the undecided items you can place once the list is complete.

YES	NO	MAYBE

Inspired Action Items

The sections below represent the primary areas in balancing life. In order to improve your satisfaction level in a specific area, create three Inspired Action items that will bring you more daily joy and move you forward in achieving your goals, dreams, intentions and desires.

Date: _____

Career & Education:
1.
2.
3.

Romantic Relationship:
1.
2.
3..

Money:
1.
2.
3.

Personal Growth:
1.
2.
3.

Health & Wellness:
1.
2.
3.

Fun & Hobbies:
1.
2.
3.

Friends & Family:
1.
2.
3.

Physical Spaces:
1.
2.
3.

Completion of Inspired Actions: _____

Wheel of Relationships

How satisfied are you in each of these areas of your relationship...right NOW, _____*? (today's date)*

The 12 sections in the Wheel of Relationship represent the areas in your life that support an integrated, balanced and interconnected relationship. Seeing the center of the wheel as 0 and the outer edge as 10, rank your level of satisfaction in each area of your relationship by drawing a line to create a new outer edge within the wheel (see sample).

Overall Relationship Satisfaction (0-10): ___

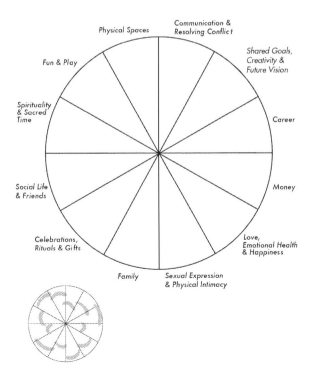

Excavating Your Best Habits

When you think about your life, what habits do you practice on a regular basis that keep you centered, grounded and focused on taking care of the most important person: YOU? List the things you are willing to do daily, weekly and monthly to take EXTREMELY good care of yourself. These can be anything from saying your morning prayers, clearing your desk at the end of the day or taking a hot bath at night to exercising three times per week, buying flowers, taking a class or connecting with someone you miss or care about each month. Make sure your new habits are things you are willing to commit to doing consistently and that you LOVE to do them, as opposed to what you think you should do. Treat yourself with enormous generosity.

DAILY
1. _____
2. _____
3. _____

WEEKLY
1. _____
2. _____
3. _____
4. _____
5. _____
6. _____
7. _____

MONTHLY
1. _____
2. _____
3. _____

Common Themes in The True You
By Chapter

Authenticity: 1, 3, 4, 7, 13, 15, 18, 24, 35, 37, 42, 46, 47, 50

Beauty & Physical Spaces: 6, 9, 18, 20, 31, 39, 43, 48

Career: 18, 32, 33, 36, 37, 38, 40, 44, 45, 48, 50

Creativity: 15, 32, 33, 45, 48, 51

Effective Communication: 1, 5, 16, 18, 22, 27, 29, 34, 35, 37, 38, 42, 46, 47, 50, 51

Emotional Clarity: 10, 11, 13, 17, 18, 20, 29, 30, 31, 39, 43, 44, 48, 49

Extreme Self-Care & Wellness: 2, 4, 5, 6, 14, 17, 24, 25, 26, 28, 30, 32, 39, 41, 43, 44, 46, 47, 48, 49

Fun & Play: 2, 14, 18, 38, 43, 45, 48, 51

Gratitude: 1, 5, 8, 16, 18, 20, 48

Healthy Relationships: 1, 7, 9, 10, 13, 15, 17, 18, 22, 24, 25, 27, 30, 31, 35, 36, 37, 43, 44, 45, 46, 48, 51, 52

Life Balance: 9, 21, 26, 28, 34, 36, 39, 45, 47, 52

Money & Abundance: 12, 31, 36, 45, 52

Moving Forward & Inspired Action: 3, 4, 16, 17, 18, 21, 23, 29, 33, 34, 38, 40, 41, 42, 45, 49, 50, 51

Organization & Time: 8, 19, 31, 37, 52

Overcoming Fear & Limitations: 4, 10, 11, 12, 18, 23, 27, 30, 35, 42, 52

Passion & Aliveness: 1, 2, 3, 15, 16, 18, 22, 25, 28, 43, 44, 46, 47, 49, 50, 51, 52

Personal Freedom: 3, 5, 10, 13, 23, 24, 27, 29, 30, 40, 51, 52

Power & Empowerment: 1, 4, 5, 6, 10, 11, 12, 16, 27, 28, 32, 33, 34, 37, 38, 49, 50, 52

Soulful Goal Setting: 9, 10, 21, 33, 38, 40, 41, 45, 47, 49, 52

Spirituality: 3, 9, 14, 16, 19, 20, 25, 27, 28, 30, 31, 39, 47, 49

About the Author

Jennifer Blair is a Life Coach, Speaker and Writer based in Louisville, Kentucky and Fort Worth, Texas. In 2003, she founded Excavive™ Life Coaching as a way to empower people, especially women, to pursue their passions, increase their self-confidence, and build the kind of lives they truly want to live.

Jennifer's passionate commitment to her work focuses on personal and professional life coaching, creative and entrepreneurial consulting, inspirational speaking, writing—and occasionally—teaching salsa dancing. Her lifelong leadership experiences, extensive coaches training through the Coaches Training Institute and public speaking are making a difference in the lives of clients and audiences all over the nation.

As a native Texan, Jennifer graduated from Southern Methodist University in Dallas and then served in various communications roles for EDS, Senator Lloyd Bentsen's office and the Louisville Bar Association. Her numerous volunteer activities have allowed her to mentor women, especially through her roles as president of The Junior League of Louisville, co-chair of the Race for the Cure- and being a mother.

Jennifer's business has continued to evolve from local one-on-one life coaching to serving clients all over the nation though several different mediums. Jennifer provides interactive and inspirational speaking for small and large groups, board trainings, non-profit organizations, universities and corporations. She writes a monthly column that focuses on in-depth life coaching issues called Evolve for *Underwired* Magazine in Louisville, and has also been tapped to provide expert interviews for KET's "Louisville Life," NPR's "State of Affairs," Vibrantnation.com, *The Voice-Tribune*, *Louisville Magazine*, *Velocity* and "All About You" radio show.

Jennifer is a member of the International Coaches Federation, the Ohio Valley Professional Coach Alliance, Louisville Coaches Connect, the Junior League of Louisville, and a co-director of Greater Louisville Outstanding Women, Inc. (GLOW).

Excavive™ Life Coaching Company

Jennifer offers several avenues for both personal and professional growth through her company, Excavive™ Life Coaching—all to help you create the life you have always wanted to live. Whether it's through the Excavive™ life coaching process of self-discovery, the inspirational speaking events and trainings, or the creative yet practical articles she has written, all services assist her clients in fiercely moving forward in their lives. She specializes in:

- Individual Life Coaching
- Life Transitions such as career, divorce or empty nesting
- Relationship Coaching
- Effective Communications
- Entrepreneurial Leadership
- Corporate Coaching
- Creativity Consulting
- Inspirational Speaking for Keynotes, Retreats, Workshops and small groups
- Freelance Writing

For a free e-mail subscription to her monthly newsletter, "Excavate Yourself" send an e-mail to info@excavive.com or sign-up directly on the web site, www.excavive.com. There are coaching tips, client success stories, my latest coaching column, upcoming appearances and additional book suggestions.

For information about speaking topics, availability and rates please visit www.excavive.com/speaking or e-mail her directly at jennifer@excavive.com.

And if you would like to know more about Life Coaching, please visit her web site, www.excavive.com/coaching or to learn if she is the right coach for you, please e-mail her directly at jennifer@excavive.com to set up a half-hour complimentary informational session.

To discover more about any of the Excavive™ Life Coaching services, visit the web site, www.excavive.com or connect directly by calling, writing or e-mailing:

Jennifer M. Blair, Owner and Life Coach
Excavive™ Life Coaching
P.O. Box 8186
Louisville, KY 40257
502.893.9589
Jennifer@excavive.com
www.excavive.com